THE PROPERTY MANAGER
MINDSET

Dormant Volcano Publishing

dormantvolcanopublishing@gmail.com

ISBN: 978-1-7771621-0-8 (print)

ISBN: 978-1-7771621-1-5(ebook)

Ordering Information:

Special discounts are available on quantity purchases by corporations,
associations, and others. For details, contact dormantvolcanopublishing@gmail.
com

TABLE OF CONTENTS

THE PROPERTY MANAGER
MINDSET

REDUCE STRESS, SAVE TIME, EARN MORE MONEY

GARY SPENCER-SMITH

INTRODUCTION

Your rental property is an investment for your future, and it has its own unique set of challenges. You have to deal with the headaches of owning and managing real estate while dealing with your tenants. It will also affect your lifestyle, and it may not be the dream you thought it was when you initially set out to buy a rental. And you are not alone! Your struggles—even though it may feel like you are the only one having them—are just part of the job. If you follow the advice in this book, it will help you to better understand and deal with the game of real estate investing.

This book is a powerful tool to help you deal with your tenants and your rental property(ies) and to help you create mutually beneficial relationships with your tenants. Mostly, it will help you to control your rental property and to make sure that your rental property or tenant doesn't control you. Real estate investing, when you do it right, should help you *live* your life, not *be* your life!

The information herein will help you understand how sophisticated real estate investors look at their investments. It is based on my many years of experience in the business, and when applied to you and your real estate, it will help you save money, reduce stress, and save your sanity by putting you control of your investments.

CHAPTER 1

HOW TO VIEW YOUR ~~TENANT~~ CLIENT

Commonly used sentences we hear all the time:

1. The problem with rental houses is dealing with tenants.
2. Tenants have all the rights.
3. Never rent to (insert race/religion/gender).

Imagine if you drove a vehicle for 10 years and then one day you got into a crash, were injured, lost income from work, had pain for a long time; and then when you got your car back, you got into *another crash* within weeks. Then *you never drove again*!

Unfortunately, this is what many landlords do–and put into context like this, it seems silly. One, two, or a few bad incidents do not outweigh the hundreds or thousands of days you have incident-free! Sure, there are a few crazy or stupid or dangerous drivers, but most are not!

When someone hears the same things spoken repeatedly, they start to believe the narrative. The trouble with a lot of the narrative is that the people speaking have had very little, or even *zero* experience. Owning one rental house and renting to a few people over five to 10 years, and then having one bad incident, is *not* experience; it's just one bad incident. Experience is regularly and repeatedly dealing successfully with incidents over a prolonged period of time.

Some landlords will have a bad incident because of how they manage their renters, or because of where the property is, or the type of person it attracts.

When people view their tenants, they literally have a preconceived notion of who they are and then call them "tenants." Imagine if you changed your description, and instead of *"tenant"* you used the word *"client."* The word "tenant" can have so many negatives attached to it: problematic, midnight phone calls; blocked toilets; and damage! The word "client" is someone who gives you money because of the service *you* provide them! This simple change in how you view your tenant will dramatically change how you deal with the people renting your investment property. Imagine if you owned a store and every month someone came in and gave you between $1,000 and $3,000—*every* month for a whole year. And *every* year that is as much as $36,000.

How important would that client be to you? What would you do for that client? How would you greet them when they entered your store? How would you deal with any issues they may have with the product they purchased? What would you do if you knew it was their birthday, or if it was Christmas time?

Now let us reframe your thinking...imagine your "client" is now the person who is renting your rental house—a box that's clean, warm, and dry.

For the use of this clean, warm, dry box, the client is going to pay you between $12,000 and $36,000 a year. Of course, you have some expenses: the purchase of your product (the mortgage), the business expenses (repairs and maintenance), accounting, staff (management costs), etc. It's not straight profit into your pocket. Some months you may even have more expenses than rent.

But, the beauty of this arrangement is that after 20 to 30 years, that mortgage will be paid off. Your customer (or a number of customers) will have paid off the mortgage on that clean, warm, dry box. Or, even better, because we're actually talking about a house and not a box, after a number of years, the home you've been renting out has had a value increase. So, your client has paid for all the repairs to your home during this period, looked after it, kept it clean, and now you get to keep those profits and value increases.

Taking this back to real estate, if your rental is worth $400,000, and the market increases by only 3 percent per year, you get to keep approximately $60,000 over a four to five-year period. But, the wonderful thing is that the value doesn't even have to increase. The same benefit occurs just from having the mortgage paid down over the same time period. This situation can be even better if you are making a *profit* and not just covering costs.

Now ask yourself the following questions:

How much do you like your "client" now?

What would you be willing to do for them now?

Is this worth sending a card during festive times to say, "Thank you"?

When things get stressful, and they will, or when things get heated due to an issue, and they will–this is the best time to ask yourself: Okay, what can I do to help my client understand and alleviate the problem? What can I do for my client to help prevent this situation from escalating? If you feel yourself still getting worked up, ask yourself: How much money has this person given me?

And what if they left my house messy, and somewhat damaged, and the repair bill is going to be somewhere between $3,000 and $6,000?

If, in the same timeframe, you have made $18,000 in profits, after mortgage paydown and cash flow have been taken into account, then *smile*–you have made money and you are in profit. After you finish smiling, arrange the repairs, clean up, and move on to find the next client who will give you $18,000 gross, minus $6,000 for repairs, for a net profit of $12,000. Do this for 20 years, and even if the house price *stays the same,* you will receive around **a quarter of a million dollars per house!**

Plus, the added bonus is that *you will now own the house* because the mortgage will be paid down. **Now do this for only four rental houses and there is your million dollars over 20 years!** If you are around 40 to 50 years old, there is your retirement! Now how important are those clients to your life? How will you treat your clients when *your* future retirement is in their hands? Many individuals and groups "sell" the get-rich-quick mentality because that's what a lot of people who are desperate about money *want.* Real estate, on the other hand, is a longer-term investment, and if you invest with that long-term mindset, then short-term "issues" will be less troublesome and your "clients" will be people you look to serve as you invest in your future.

Can you see how even thinking of the person as a "client" instead of a "tenant" will make you view the whole situation from a different perspective? It will also help you to stay accountable for *your* actions in the scenario, which is a lot easier than thinking you can control the other person. It will help you to keep your sanity, be a better landlord, and differentiate yourself from the crowd.

At the beginning of the chapter, we stated what people often say. Now that we have a different perspective, those statements will also change....

From "The problem with rental houses is dealing with tenants" **to** "Clients are the lifeblood of my business; how can I improve myself and my service to them?"

From "Tenants have all the rights" **to** "I work with my clients to build relationships and find solutions."

From "Never rent to (*insert race/religion/gender*)" **to** "I have all different types of clients who spend their hard-earned money in my business and I value all of them."

CHAPTER 2

ARE ~~TENANTS~~ CLIENTS *NUTS?*
UNDERSTANDING THE "TENANT"
MENTALITY AND HOW THEY THINK

~Not All Tenants Are Created Equal.~

You may often view others as you view yourself, and then when people do not think as you do, or how you expect them to, you get annoyed and stressed. Is this their fault or yours? Depending on where you are renting and what you are renting, your tenant profile is going to change–and this change can be dramatic, even one block away. Have you ever heard parents say–or even if you have your own kids, have you ever said, "My kids are total opposites" or "They are nothing like each other!"? Duh! Of course, they are different!

Newsflash: every person is different, and because every person is different, it makes sense to say that every tenant will be different. How, then, can you get mostly consistent results over the duration of your property investing adventure if all the people you deal with are very different from one another?

Different "groups" of people

Even though every person is different, there are "types" of people; different classes and groups and if you can understand them, and how they think and operate, you will be able to meet their expectations, and *they will be able to meet yours*. Whenever our company advertises, or conducts a phone interview, or meets people at a viewing, we *grade* the potential tenants and categorize them into A, B, or C. That's right…we judge! And you should too!

To explain what the categories are:

A is the top category. They did exactly as you asked in the advert (more about this later), showed up early, presented themselves well, and all their references checked out as highly positive. They have secure jobs, an excellent history, and are well paid – which you verify with due diligence, like confirming payslips and with employers. They are also well-dressed and have great communication skills—written, on the phone, and in person. These factors and their personal traits show me that they deserve to be in the top tier. When *you* start being judgemental and grading people, you will also want to use these same standards.

B level, as you can guess, is a step down from A. It is *never* anything personal and I don't allow my personal prejudices (we all have them in one way or another, whether consciously or unconsciously) to cloud my decision (and you should not let them cloud yours either). B typically doesn't have the history that A has, may earn a little less or be a little less refined, may not communicate quite as clearly as A, and/or perhaps did not follow up on *all* the things I requested in the application. They will typically still have a solid income and be respectful of themselves, their belongings, and others. About 80 percent of the rentals you will own or manage will fall into this category due to the fact that this is most of the population (depending on your rental location).

C level, for want of a better description, may be a little rougher around the edges. That is, perhaps they didn't communicate in the way you had requested; they may have shown up and been a little less well-presented or prepared; they may have very little or no previous rental history; and perhaps they just moved to the country and/or just started renting because they are young.

If they are a **level D** or below, I simply do not rent to them. Period. It's nothing personal; I just do not want to deal with the issues that come with that market. Typically, these would be "shady" characters, people who may have substance abuse issues, people who have a poor job history, etc. There is a lot of opportunity in renting to level D or below. However, for me, not renting to level D is a personal preference; and if you want to remain hassle-free, and minimize your headaches when it comes to your rentals, you should also avoid this category!

Giving them your rental, regardless of how big a sob story they have, is *not* going to help you. If you decide to operate in this category, and many do, understand that these renters come with a very specific set of challenges, and you have to be willing to deal with them. Some of the challenges include: the use of various drugs; undesirable friends and roommates coming and going; very poor upkeep on the property, meaning you will need to spend on repairs; difficulty making the rent payments.

If you already have a level-D rental, buy indestructible flooring and appliances, or very cheap ones and replace regularly. And find furniture that fits the situation. Again, these are just a few things to highlight some of the extra challenges if you decide to operate in this category. However, if you are reading this book, you probably won't.

So why categorize tenants into groups A, B, and C? Because it gives you the ability to ensure that you are getting the tenants you want *and*, most importantly, that you match the right tenants to the right house. That's right—you should grade your properties A, B, and C. The properties we manage all get graded as A, B, or C.

You can grade your properties as A if they are magazine-style homes, pristine homes, manicured lawns and gardens, or beautiful condos in new buildings with all the trimmings. Granite countertops, gorgeous floors, or a brand-new home in a highly desirable area.

B homes are the nicer builder-grade homes; or perhaps a slightly older home that has had a complete renovation and upgrades; or a mid-age home built in the late '90s or early 2000s, so it may be a little dated but it is still a good home that people will enjoy. As for the area, it might be a little less desirable but still a good place to bring up your kids.

C homes are your older homes, well built, attractive, and comfortable, but may have some dated areas, perhaps a bathroom that's older, or a kitchen that could do with an update—think '70s or '80s style homes. They function well, everything works, but it's just a little older. The area will be okay but it may be a place where you might not want your kids playing on the street, or it's a busy road or something like that.

Always place an A person in an A house—or *below if that's what they* want. B group people are always placed in B group houses or possibly C group houses, but *never* put C tenants in an A group house or a B group house. C group people are placed in C group houses *only*.

We have a whole system that helps us grade the houses, and also checklists to ensure that they are graded correctly and that it's not just someone's personal opinion. This helps to take the emotion out of the equation and the decision. (If you register this book on our website, we will give you access to these checklists.)

Where grading tenants and properties can create conflict is when an owner or joint venture partner "*believes*" the property is above the level that we would assign to the property. For example, they believe their property is a B or A when really it is a C, and they only want A tenants. Usually A tenants will not want to be in a C house, and if they are in one, they will move at the earliest opportunity when an A house becomes available. It is beneficial to match the correct tenants to the correct houses if you want longer-term tenants who will respect the house and treat it the way it should be treated.

A and B tenants typically do not respect a C property as much as they would an A or B property. Likewise, a C tenant will not look after an A or a B house the way you would want them to. This is one of the most important lessons to prevent unexpected issues. Grading tenants and properties also ensures your decisions are based on *process* rather than *emotion*. You still want to let your gut help guide you, especially if something does not "feel right" and you are unable to verify the information you are given, or even find any information. Matching the right tenants to the right houses is *crucial* to your long-term success, and choosing the right tenants to have as your clients is the most important factor in your role as a rental-housing provider. Also note that this is the time when you have the most power and control over your property.

Now to help you differentiate: An A tenant would be the kind of person who, even despite a conflict between homeowner and tenant, would leave it the same as, or if not better than, when they moved in. B would have generated a bit of wear and tear and maybe not done a perfect clean-up; and C would have more wear and tear and more clean-up to be done. Again, this does not mean you don't rent to B or C. It just means you *know* what you are getting into, and what you are most likely going to have to rectify at move-out time. Knowledge allows you to prepare and plan.

I saw a question in a Facebook group called *Landlords Anonymous BC*, which asked: When moving out, what are some of the biggest lies a tenant has told you? There were lots of stories, some funny and some not so funny, but when I thought about it, I realized the biggest and most common lie that I receive is: **"It's clean!"** I laugh when I hear this. Most of the rentals in our portfolio of currently over 60 rentals are B group properties and tenants, with a few A, and a few C, so I always expect, at the very least, that we will have to do a deep clean and polish. I do, on a few occasions, have to do much more, but at times, I'm pleasantly surprised because after all, not all tenants are created equally and when you match the right house to the right person, the results for you and your business will be extremely positive more often!

So how do you assess a property to see if it has value, and/or opportunity, and then grade it correctly? First, there are a few rules I follow in my assessments that determine its grade, and if I am going to dig further than a glance and potentially buy it. Is it in the area I want to own in, and are the tenants in this area the profile I want to deal with? Is it an A house in an A area where A tenants want to live? If I bought it now, as is, and rented it out tomorrow, does it cash flow? Cash flow is your profit after *all* the bills are paid. Or at the very least, does it cover its own cost? Below are some of these costs:

- Mortgage–always go a couple of percentages *above* to allow for changes
- Insurance
- Taxes
- City utilities–water, garbage, sewer, etc.
- Maintenance (we allow 5 percent of gross income)
- Utilities, if included
- Property Management (even if you're doing it yourself, pay yourself the same rate)
- Vacancy allowance (we allow 8 percent of gross income).

After all these expenses, will the market rental in this area cover these costs and still have profit left over? If it will, then I will take a further look and consider grading the property.

On my second look, I consider two things:

What grade would I really put this house into?

The one percent rule. For every $100,000 spent, can I get $1,000 of income, or very close to it? In today's market, that ratio can be very hard to find, but as a starting point it allows you to very quickly assess properties and compare apples to apples.

With 20 percent down, can I make 10 percent cash-on-cash profit annually? For example: A $300,000 house = $60,000 down. Can I get $3,000 of rent from the property or close to it? And after *all* the expenses are accounted for, does it make $6,000 per year positive cash flow? So, $500 per month cash flow in this scenario.

I have a spreadsheet, which I acquired from the Real Estate Intelligence Network through my membership and when I put the numbers in, it shows me on a chart if I am easily going to meet those targets or not. In the illustration below, landing underneath the lower line is great, but I would still question why the value of the home is so *low* or why the rent is so *high* compared to the price. Between the two lines is good on all accounts; nearer the upper line means more caution, and nearer the lower line is better.

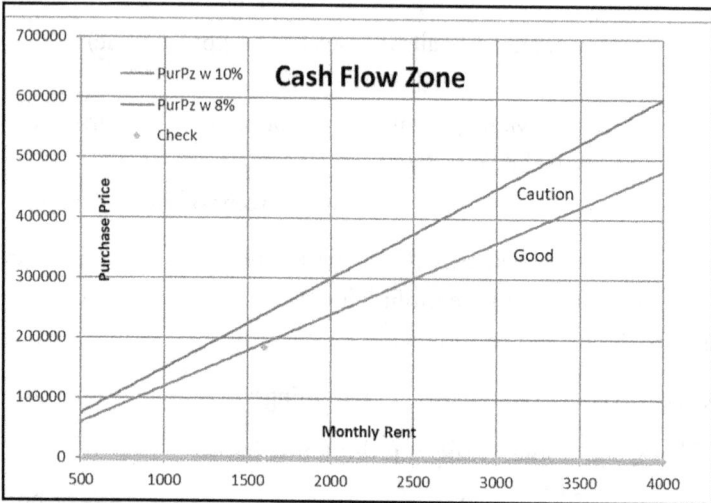

(Chart Courtesy or REIN Cash flow analyzer)

This does not mean the property will cash flow every month if something happens, but is it possible? If it meets these two criteria, I consider viewing it. At the viewing, this is where you can decide if there is a way to create more value for the property, such as adding a suite, adding a garage, etc. Or is it a B property in an A area and some upgrades would make it an A house? One thing to be very wary of here is: Even if the numbers make sense, is the house an A house in a B or C area? If it is an A in a B or C area, you will struggle to find A tenants who want to live in a B or C area!

Before viewing

Before viewing, do a financial assessment to look at extra expenses not accounted for above. These include:

- Vacancy rate: Always allow a percentage, so when it happens–and it will–it's already covered. We allow for 8 percent of the rent (which equals one month's vacancy a year, even if vacancy is below this).
- Maintenance, strata, or emergency fund: Again, build it up *ahead* of the time when you need it, so it's accounted for without hassle or headache when it is needed. And it *will* be!
- Accounting cost: Make sure the house pays for itself and that nothing comes out of your pocket.

I have spreadsheets that create an analysis of the house. I get mine from the Real Estate Intelligence Network (REIN Canada)—another benefit of joining a group where people have experience that you can mine and then modify to suit your needs. I originally made my own spreadsheets, but I found that when I needed advice, I had to explain my work. So, I changed over to one that other people used, so I could have conversations with them while I was learning, and so we were all "singing off the same hymn sheet." Again, added value to your time and expenditure.

When you use spreadsheets, it also removes the speculation and emotion that we all go through (including you) in our heads when we want something. This way, we get an unbiased reference point on a chart or spreadsheet that allows us to make an educated decision. Sometimes it feels like I keep entering data and a house will never meet the criteria–which is happening now in today's market; then at other times it seems like every house fits the criteria. Just because you want to buy at a certain time in a certain market, *doesn't* mean that you *should*! If the data is showing you no, then no!

Buying right and grading right–the easiest way to eliminate headaches and stress, and to create value.

Perhaps look at what you want to buy, where you want to buy, and then ask yourself what your goal is for having real estate. The benefits of owning real estate, the gains, the upsides, and does it meet the guidelines you have set to prevent you from buying a lemon?

As for me personally, I have owned at one end of the country and lived at the other and been totally hands-off. When I had a "job," this was great. Now I have a company that works with other investors whom we partner with to create joint ventures. We renovate and manage the properties and tenants; I deal in areas that I can drive to and that provide the returns that meet my criteria. This is now my full-time job and we have staff to help us, so it is okay for me to deal with things as I have the time. This is my business. If you have a working life already, do you want dealing with real estate to be part of that?

I still outsource a lot of the work to subcontractors; however, they work for us and we control their actions. You have to decide *how you want to operate.* Do you want to be hands-on? Do you want to do your day job, and then come home and deal with housing issues? Because when things are not going as well as they should be, your time can get taken up very quickly.

Or would you rather pay the money and have someone else do the work for you, deal with the headaches, do all the due diligence and calculations, and then give you a pro-forma sheet? In this scenario, you remain hands-off but still reap 50-60 percent of all the profits. If this is what you would prefer, find someone who is experienced and with whom you can joint venture. If you can't find anyone, we just might do it for you! This opens up your ability to own in multiple areas if you wish, or to focus on an area further away that provides better returns than your local market. It also reduces stress for you when you do not have to deal with the day-to-day of running around, making phone calls, and dealing with disgruntled tenant issues. Either way, you need to decide who you are, what you want, and then look at a property to make sure it meets your needs over time and takes you closer to your goals.

Tenant mentality and homeowner mentality—how it affects your judging ability

Another *huge* mistake you will see owners making when qualifying clients for their rental units is thinking that tenants are just like *them*, and that tenants think just like *they* do! Then they get stressed or p***ed off when their tenants are not like them at all! Let me make this as crystal clear as I can: 99 percent of tenants are *tenants*; they are **not** *homeowners*. They do not think like homeowners; and they do not behave like homeowners; because—yes, you guessed it—they are *not* homeowners!

I ask my coaching clients this all the time: as a homeowner, if something breaks, what's your first thought? Yes, that's right, you've got to fix it or get it fixed. For tenants, the typical first thought when something breaks is: "I've got to call the landlord and report it" (hopefully). Or they think: "F**k it. It's not my problem!"

I know this sounds super harsh, and I want it to—because tenants do not think like *you*. And to take it a step further, homeowners like yourself who start to buy rentals, and instantly become "investors" and business owners, need to shift your mentality. You do not *yet* think like investors and business owners. So, when a homeowner like you buys a rental unit because you believe rentals are a good investment, you are not yet an investor or even a business owner or property manager, because you haven't even managed any properties yet. You think like homeowners, because you *are* one!

So, when you are qualifying clients for your rental business, understand that you need to have a mind shift when you are evaluating them. If you have a different mindset, you will have different expectations, and when these do not get met, you get upset because they do not think the same as you. They also have a very different mindset, and a different set of expectations, and because of that difference that is what causes stress and other negative emotions, which only serves to harm you! Shift your understanding and your mindset to understand *their* mindset, and you do this to reduce your stress and understand the picture from a different viewpoint. "The best way to catch a crook is to think like a crook!"

Here is an example of the tenant/homeowner mentality and how it can affect your stress levels:

The Margaret story

Let us call her Margaret to keep her identity safe. Margaret had a home. She owned this home and lived in it for many years, and then she decided to sell it to her daughter. She moved out and bought a new home, and her daughter took over the house and paid all the bills. Now for a few years this was hassle-free—it was her daughter, she knew what she was getting, they understood the mindset and expectations of each other, and all was good. Then one day her daughter decided to move after she split from her husband. The market wasn't great for selling, so Margaret thought: "*I know, I'll rent it out.*" The house was a single-family home in a decent area and under my grading system it was a B class home. Nice, but it needed some work and it was a little tired around the fringes. We helped Margaret find some B class tenants and they moved in.

During their two years there, they always paid the rent and all the bills; sometimes it was late by a few days, but they *always paid*.

They let the yard go a bit as they were not gardeners like the previous owner; however, they mowed the lawns and kept it looking okay. Margaret, still thinking of this as her home, and thinking like a homeowner, wished they were more like she was. And the tenants, thinking like tenants, were sometimes frustrated by Margaret's meddling, which caused some conflict between the two but nothing serious. It was more like they just didn't like each other.

After two years, Margaret's daughter decided she wanted to move back into the house. Notice was served to the tenants, despite their having recently signed a new two-year lease, with a well-above-the-allowed-increase on rent—at the tenants' request—so they could get a longer-term contract as they knew what was happening in the market. Truly upset, since they had planned their life around staying in this property, they now had to find a new place to live in a very tight market.

The local rules in British Columbia, for example, dictate that when serving notice for the landlord's use of the property, a two-month notice is given, and either the last month's rent is refunded, *or* they get the last month's rent free. This helps them to put down a deposit on a new place and cover the costs of being forced to move.

They were given more than two months to move, and Margaret had said she didn't want them to leave before a certain date since that was when her daughter was moving in. We explained that she couldn't ask them to leave and then dictate what date they should move out! In the end, they found a home, took it, and left a month before Margaret wanted them to. They also chose to take the last month rent-free instead of paying and having it refunded. Due to the way things went, they also decided not to clean and they signed to say keep the deposit, since they felt Margaret was going to be keeping it anyway. Margaret got upset and her words to us were: "What, so now I get stiffed on the last month's rent, too?!"

We were shocked, and we informed Margaret that she had in fact asked them to move out in a tight market. We explained that they might not have been able to find a home, and then they would have been stuck in the house, and possibly we would have had to get a possession order, which can take months. We also explained that during their time in the house, they had paid down approximately $15,000 of mortgage on top of the profit the house made every month.

When her daughter got to the house, yes, it was worn—it needed paint, the carpets needed to be cleaned, and some dump runs would be necessary—and she started to complain about the time it was going to take to fix it up. We explained that she had the deposit, which the tenant had agreed she could keep—and she could use that to pay someone to do the work. In the end she chose to do it herself and keep the money, but still complained that she had to do it.

The cost of all the work to be done, due to the condition of the carpets and the painting requirements, was going to exceed the amount of deposit the tenant had left. However, based on the concepts in the previous paragraphs, even if the cleaning cost more than the deposit, they should have been asking themselves: How much has my client paid me and what is my *profit* versus the small expense it is costing right now?

In total, they were about $20,000 better off at the end of the term, and instead of being angry, they should have been smiling, saying thank you, and buying the client a leaving present. Instead they chose to stay angry and bitter. Who suffers in this scenario? A slight change in the way they viewed the whole situation would have helped them to complete the process, wish their client the best, and allowed them to stay calm and happy.

When choosing your clients to tenant your property, if you have the mindset and understanding of who *they* are **and** who *you* are in the overall scenario, it will help you make better decisions and understand the perspectives of both you as the owner and the tenant as your client.

As you can see, tenants are *not* homeowners, and they do not think like homeowners because they have a different mindset. And most homeowners with rentals, like you, do not think like investors, just like Margaret didn't because that was her mindset! *You* have to shift *your* thinking in order to reduce stress on yourself. If Margaret had understood the tenant mentality, and also understood her mentality as an investor and not just as a homeowner, she would have been far less stressed and upset about the whole situation.

How could grading tenants have had an impact on this situation? If Margaret had understood the concept of grading tenants, and therefore understood what to expect from the end of this particular tenancy (all tenancies end at some point), she would have been prepared. Knowing what to expect would have reduced her "expectations" and therefore reduced the stress that she experienced afterwards. Now ask yourself, how would different grades of tenants been at the end of this tenancy?

CHAPTER 3

YOU ARE PERFECT *(NOT)* — KNOW THYSELF!

Who You Are and Why It Matters—Become the Person that Attracts Success in Rentals

We all like to think of ourselves as pretty amazing, as almost perfect, and as having the ability to deal with anything or anyone. The truth is, there are very few of us out there who are perfect. Of course, I'm joking with that sentence—*no one* is perfect.

All joking aside, it is imperative to understand who you are, who you are when dealing with tenants/clients, and who you are in stressful situations, such as the police showing up at your rental. How do you react when there are arguments between neighbours at your rentals or you receive a phone call from the neighbours telling you that your rental is on fire? Or when your tenant tells you something and you know for a fact that they are 100 percent lying? Or when you receive threats of violence, late payments when all the bills are due, or late payments when you see on Facebook that they have new tattoos, concert tickets, and new cars? Or they have multiple people living in your rental when you rented to only one or two people? And how do you react when you have to deal with a leaky roof; rats chewing through water pipes and causing floods; collapsed perimeter drains, and always on the wettest, rainiest days; piles of garbage left after moving out; furniture left; drugs left; even pets left?

All of these have happened to us, and more! Each time we looked at who we had been in the situation, and what we could have done differently; and most importantly, what lessons did we learn? That approach will help you to be even more successful as a landlord. Each time there is an incident, ask yourself what can you learn from this, and what can you do or improve to make sure it doesn't happen again? Learning is growth; the more you grow, the better you become, and the more money your business will make.

We could scare you with stories from the battlefield; however, we have *never* lost out financially on our return on investments with a rental property. Learning to understand yourself better, and to thoroughly understand the business, will help you put more money in your pocket. We have never been in the red due to any of these things, and we will help you to ensure that you have the same positive results, even when you encounter your own battle-field stories. We have stories about how we dealt with and overcame *all of them*, but the biggest deciding factor in how you will deal with any of the dramas above is who you are as a person when dealing with your tenants or clients.

Twenty-five years ago, I was not the person I am today, and back then, if I had been in a position to deal with some of the situations mentioned above, and some of the people, I probably would have been hauled away on assault charges because I was confrontational and hotheaded! Thankfully, by the time I had to face these challenges, I had developed a set of skills that enabled me to cope and to manage the issues. Those skills included self-control, the ability to see things from another perspective, people management skills, organizational skills, and business management skills.

I wish I could say I did it all with a smile, but I'd be lying. I have a smile on my face looking back, but at the time I felt the same emotions that most of you will—anger, frustration, sadness, guilt, loss, bewilderment, and outright being flabbergasted. Understanding what your skill set is or is not will be highly valuable when you plan how to deal with various circumstances. And if you do not have certain skills, know what those are so you can hire the right people to help you with those situations. And you can work on developing those skills so you can become an even more successful real estate investor and landlord. Of course, skills can be developed, but first you have to learn what you have, and more importantly what you need.

Knowing yourself puts you in a better position to deal with rentals and the tenants that occupy them. Are you the kind of person that would "throat punch" someone if they did not do as you ask? (My other half is that person.) And if you *are* that person too, then you need to know what you should and should *not* be dealing with in order to prevent an unsavoury incident. Knowing your limits allows you to hire, train, or plan in order to prevent any situations where you "might" throat punch someone. Throat punches to clients never end well for the landlord! In fact, I think it's against most tenancy laws!

This could be one of the most important chapters for you. If you think you could *not* cope if any or all of the above incidents happened to you, then perhaps you need to hire someone who has the skills, someone who can manage your property for you. Is a couple of thousand dollars a year worth having no headaches at all when you're making $30,000-$50,000–plus a year from a rental property? This is a decision only you can make based on the type of person you are.

Here are a few questions to learn what you would you do if the following happened to your rental, your investment, and your future. Really think about each question, perhaps even write down the answers. But if you don't have the answers, that's okay too, because you can always ask someone who has experienced these challenges and achieved positive results. Let that be the start of your own "policies and procedures manual"!

Ask yourself how you would react and what you would do if:

1. **The house caught on fire.**
2. **The tenant came out and aggressively threatened you.**
3. **The tenant physically assaulted you.**
4. **The tenant laughed at you when the rent hadn't been paid, and you now must pay the difference to pay the bills.**
5. **You renovated the house and now you look through the window and see nothing but mess and damage.**
6. **You have pest problems—raccoons, rats, bats....**
7. **Every time you drive by, the yard is a mess and the grass needs cutting.**
8. **The tenant you rented to has moved out and someone else is living there.**
9. **Someone dies in your rental.**
10. **Someone kills himself in your rental.**
11. **Vermin chew through your water lines and the basement suite floods.**
12. **A single parent hasn't paid rent for nearly two months, and you have notice for possession and must tell him**

or her that they have two days to leave before bailiffs arrive.

13. You find out the tenant or their older teenage child is dealing illegal drugs.

14. Crazy neighbours move in and they harass your great tenants, making up stories and relaying them to the city to cause trouble.

15. A bylaw officer is on your case, despite the fact that the tenancy laws prohibit you from taking action.

If you answered the above questions as you went through, that's great; write them down in a binder, a "what if" binder if you want to call it that. Then think about anything else that "could" happen and write that down too. Now below each "what if," write down the answers—the steps you would take to resolve the issues; and if you don't know the answer, ask someone who has experienced the problem and ended up with a positive outcome. Ask how they did it and what actions they took. That way, when you come across these problems in your own life—and let's hope you never do, but if you *do*—you will have a set of systems and processes to refer to.

We all get upset and angry at things that happen to us; it's how we react to these emotions and feelings that determines the outcome and the results. You want to ensure that your reactions and actions end up with positive results for you. So, know yourself, and when you are in a positive state of mind, ask experienced people how they have dealt with various situations (make sure they have had *success* dealing with these types of problems) and write down their answers. Eventually you will have your own "when the shit hits the fan manual" and inside will be the steps you need to take to remedy the situation, regardless of how you are "feeling" and what emotional state you are in when the incident takes place.

I would strongly recommend, if you have one rental or 100, that you work on this over time. If you want a starting point, you can download a basic format to help you get started with some step-by-step procedures.

This is a *must* for any successful rental housing provider and something that is *not* done by the average investor. If you want to be above average, to achieve above average results, and to achieve exceptional results, then you need exceptional systems and processes. And this is how you start to develop your own systems and processes, created especially for you.

Sometimes it's hard for us to admit that we might just be a bit anal about things, and other people (our clients) might not give the same kind of care that we do to the same things. Understanding this, and understanding how you will react to this, will help you prepare for whatever your rental throws at you. If it's something you haven't experienced before, learn from it, add it to your manual, and try not to repeat the same mistake! This is important growth for you, and it's important for your business and for *your peace of mind!*

Do you really know your personality? Circle the words below to see who you are. Then copy the list and give it to someone you know, asking them to circle the ones that *they* would pick to describe who you are. We often deceive ourselves regarding who we are! Understanding who you truly are will help you manage your responses to a tenant. For example, if you're frugal, does that mean you buy the cheapest fixtures, and then wonder why they keep breaking, all the while blaming the tenant for not looking after things properly? If your tenant calls to ask for something to be fixed and your response is to get aggressive and the tenant becomes confrontational, what then? Conversely, if you're compassionate and empathetic, how will you react when the "sob stories" come out (and they always do). This little exercise will help you identify who you are, and once you know and understand who you are, you can then plan how you would deal with, or react to, certain incidents. *Knowing thyself* is powerful, and it will help *you* to achieve more positive results, more of the time.

For each one that you circle (below), ask yourself how that will affect your behavior when dealing with the issues from the previous list, or anything else that might arise from the rental or the tenant.

Circle who you are and add any others that describe you at the bottom:

Happy	Sad	Outgoing	Introverted
Organized	Disorganized	Relaxed	Uptight
Short-fused	Patient	Passive	Aggressive
Frugal	Generous	Adaptable	Close-Minded
Compassionate	Hard-hearted	Diligent	Lazy

Another five words that describe you:

_____

_____

_____

_____

Write down all the behavioral traits you possess, and then assess how you will react with those traits in different scenarios. For example, if you're angry or short-fused, then you need to have in your systems—which you will develop—a reminder to walk away and call back when you've calmed down. You could choose to communicate via letters where you have time to read what is being put down before reacting. You can have someone else check an issue so you don't say or do anything that will get you into trouble or cost you money, or both!

There are things you can do to help you, and who you are, remember you are now a business owner, an investor, and a property manager and have clients just because you bought a rental or a home with a rental suite in it!

Treating tenants as clients helps *you* deal with your stress management. As with any business, you need clients to be successful; without them, your rental home, just like any business, would fail. Be good to your clients; they are the lifeblood of your business. As with any business, your clients may sometimes cause temporary problems or be difficult to deal with. If it was a store, you could think of them as the one-in-10, or one-in-20, difficult clients. Eventually they will leave that store (just like a tenant will leave your rental), and the only person who suffers if you stay annoyed with a client is *you!* Clients come in all shapes and sizes and personalities. When you know they are a client, and that your business success depends on your clients, this will help you to figure out how to deal with situations where a client is difficult, and this issue *will* appear from time to time.

Top questions to ask before dealing with a client in a stressful situation:

1. Is this going to help you moving forward and will it benefit the relationship?

2. What is the result you are trying to achieve, and are your actions going to help you to achieve it?

3. If you need to remove the client from your property, are you going to be better off financially because of this experience (in the whole picture, not just that month)? Put a number to it, and this number might be bigger than you think. Include cash flow, mortgage paydown, home appreciation. This will help you to deal with it from a different perspective, i.e., when the tenant leaves, even if evicted or if he does a "midnight move," and it costs you $4,000 in expenses, but you made $16,000 in profits, then you have profited from that client, and you own a business, so don't let it upset you!

4. Is there anything you can do to prevent the situation from escalating further?

5. Why did this happen in the first place, and what could *you* have done to prevent it?

6. Also, what can *you* do to improve in the future and ensure that this doesn't happen again?

Do you ever work on your professional development?

"What does that have to do with managing rental houses?" I hear you say.

Managing rental houses is your business and your profession, and every individual in business and in a profession needs to set aside time and energy for professional development. Do you actively work on improving your skills, and network with people who are also involved in the real estate game, including those who have more experience than you? Do you actively seek out best practices and solutions regarding things that may happen in the 25+ years that you may be investing in real estate? Or are you simply *reac-*

tive when something happens? Or are you the person that either watched a TV show about rentals, or went to a free seminar that "hyped" up the benefits of real estate and you thought why not and jumped in? Whichever way led you to your current business and profession is neither good nor bad. You just need to know who you are, because knowing who you are will help you make educated choices about whether or not you have the experience and skill set to make the best decisions for the most positive outcome when dealing with tenants.

There are many avenues to help you with your professional and personal development, and in the last chapter we have some references and guidelines that can help you. For my personal development, I started with free meet-up groups regarding real estate investing, and I started to get a different perspective than what the media or friends and family had portrayed. Then I started paying for smaller memberships that would help me, like landlord groups where I could get good advice. Then as my business grew, I started getting coaches to help me with each aspect of my business and my life around real estate investing. In hindsight, I could have saved years of time and tens of thousands of dollars had I invested in a coach sooner, but that was a lesson I had to learn.

For example, I remember taking on my first serious coach. I had read books, taken courses, knew quite a few "how-to" strategies, and even owned a few rentals; yet I felt that I still wasn't achieving the results I thought I should be achieving. I paid the sum of $2,000 (which I thought was a lot of money) to have four one-hour sessions with this coach, where he would look at what I was doing and then tell me what to do or not to do.... Or so I thought!

The whole first two sessions with him were about really digging into my "*why.*" Not the *why* I was working in real estate but the *why* I was getting out of bed—my true core beliefs. Only then did he work with me to help me create a plan that fit with my core beliefs and the life I was trying to create. If I can share anything from that eye-opening experience, it was the clarity that the coach gave me regarding my *plan*—a plan that worked for me *my way*, *where* I wanted to do it, and *what* work I would do. He wasn't selling me a particular type of strategy; he helped me to discover my purpose and then to create a plan around my purpose, using real estate as the vehicle.

With this clarity, I became super focused, stopped looking for the latest and best shiny technique that would get me there, and I went to work. A very short time after this, I truly started to see the fruits of my labour and I created a multi-million-dollar rental portfolio. It made that $2,000 investment seem so tiny in comparison to the results I achieved because of it.

A good coach isn't there to sell you something, but to help you discover, within yourself, what you want, and then to figure out, with their guidance, how to achieve it. Sure, there were some tweaks to my plan, based on their perspective and experience, but it was *my* plan. Just like your favorite food, or your ideal day—it's about *you*, not them, and a great coach helps you see that. When I now coach people regarding real estate, we spend all the early time discovering their "why"; we help them figure out what their perfect day looks like and then we see how real estate can help them achieve that. Only when they have that figured out do we talk about any real estate strategies!

If you are disorganized, then take some organization courses, or go to *messymanager.com* and download the free book from JG Francoeur, or on YouTube, watch channels from successful real estate investors. If you are angry as a person or quick to lose your temper, perhaps take some anger management courses, or learn to look through another real estate investor's rose-tinted glasses—that is, someone who views things differently than you do, so you do not get as angry when certain "situations" arise.

Ultimately, you want to always be growing and improving yourself because it will have a direct result on the outcome of your real estate investing business; and the better *you* become, the better your business becomes; and the better your business becomes, the more *money* you have to live the life you love!

CHAPTER 4

AVOID SHITTY TENANTS

In a previous chapter, we discussed grading your tenants as A, B, or C, and how to grade houses and tenants. Now we want to delve into another art form that is crucial to a successful business relationship regarding your rental property: "screening."

People get desperate when they have no one in their property and they are paying two mortgages. If they do not have any prospective clients, they start doing crazy things like putting their rental up for a "sale" price instead of market value, which costs them thousands of dollars over time. Or worse, they put in clients without screening them properly. I have known many people who have done this (including myself), and 99 percent of the time it has cost them thousands to remove these bad renters from their units. Within the last two months, I have helped two clients remove unsavoury renters from their rental units. In the most recent one, the renters were in there for a week and it cost the owner $2,600, not to mention the lost rent for two months (another $3,600). And if that is not enough reason to screen properly, then imagine the stress she put herself under during this time! And *all* of it could have been prevented if the prescreening had been done properly.

We want you to understand that in most housing provider–client relationships, *before* the tenant moves in is the time you still have power and full control! Re-read that and understand the importance of it!

As a person who was really keen to get a property filled and before I had the experience I have now, I had placed an advert, the tenant had responded as I asked (we get more into this below), all the details were there, and they sounded awesome. We spoke on the phone and they had great manners and seemed to be the ideal tenant.

Then I thought that I might as well Google them and see what came up, as well as do a court search. I was shocked! This polite, well-presented "family" woman had a rap sheet as long as Al Capone—for multiple frauds, violent attacks on people and law officers, drug offences, thefts, and numerous other misdemeanours. The Google search also showed up several interesting links, all with her picture from various social media, some with the alias names she used, and people complaining publicly about things she had done to them. Sure, she could have turned over a new leaf, but did I want to take the chance. Would you? Prescreening is the only time that *you* have full control over who you place into your investment.

When does prescreening start?

Prescreening your tenants starts *before you even speak to a tenant*. This may sound like a crazy idea, but it starts the second you look at a property before you even buy it.

Googling a property before you even look at it is also a great idea. Imagine if you didn't, and then you bought it—decent area, right price, etc.—and then found out some bad things had happened there, and it had a stigma. It would become harder to rent. I have had people who own a five-bedroom house with a full basement who say they only want to rent to a couple or to people with one kid. Who typically wants a five-bedroom house? Usually not a professional couple! Have a think about who wants to live in that area and what it is near, not who you *want* to put in your house because you bought it there. *Put your client's needs first*—this will help you decide if the property is right for the type of people you want to deal with. Ask yourself: would the type of people I want to deal with be the people who would *want* to live in this area? Is this the type of house they would want to live in? Does it have the things they would use in the immediate area? For example: gyms, schools, supermarkets, coffee shops, transport links, parks, trails, ski hills, proximity to work, and any other things the type of client you want to deal with would want.

How do you know what type of tenant you want to rent to? How do you discover this? Sometimes this is done by trial and error. For example, you rent to a group of students and then get your student rental back with holes in the wall and bathrooms that look like they came out of a war zone. Then you decide you are *never* renting to students again, but you have a house in the perfect student rental area!

If you are unsure what types of tenant profile you want to deal with, write down the different types and make a list of the pros and cons for each. They *all* have pros and cons, and if you are unsure what they are, *ask* other investors what their pros and cons are. But keep in mind that these are their opinions and not necessarily the facts, Also, who they are personally, and their ability to deal with situations associated with this type of tenant, might be different than yours. Remember: know thyself! It will help you to at least know what you *don't* want! Eventually you will be left with what you *do* want.

Now, what if you already *own* the property and you are unable to get the tenant profile you want? For example, you have a larger home that would normally appeal to a bunch of students. But they would turn that house into a party house. So now you realize that you want to work with clients who are professionals, or you just want one family to live in that property. If you already own it, ask yourself if you can change how it is used. Can you change the profile of the house and therefore who the client will be? In the case of the five-bedroom house, we helped the owner develop a plan to repurpose the house, and they turned it into a two-bedroom suite downstairs with a three-bedroom unit upstairs. So, the tenant profile changed for each unit. The owners now have better tenants and way more rent!

Ask someone with experience in the area, i.e., local experts who invest in, and have tenants in, the area. As for Realtors, as much as we have them on our power team and use them, Realtors will want to *sell* you a house, so remember that! Ask them who will *rent* in the area, and what they want if they do. Parking? A fenced yard? Access to shops and transit? By answering these questions, you will start to build a profile, and by building a profile you are screening your potential tenants.

The second step is writing the advert.

Rental adverts—writing a compelling and successful rental ad

When vacancy is low, we all look great, but when it is *not*, what can we do? This helpful "cheat sheet" will help you fill your vacancies quicker; help you to get more responses; and ultimately help you to get more $$ for your rentals ahead of everyone else.

Headline: A great ad starts with a headline. Make sure the city/town is in the headline of the advert. (This also helps when people Google search).

Example: "Spectacular modern and luxurious 3-bedroom family home in Surrey"

Body: Most adverts are like this:

"Three-bedroom home, in town, $1,500 pm plus utilities, available next month, call xxxxxx to arrange a viewing." There may be a longer few sentences here or not, and a little more body, but for the most part it is text like this.

Now, write the body like this:

*"This spectacular, modern, (*use feature from title*), large, new, 3-bedroom family home has the following features:*

- *BRAND NEW kitchen*
- *Brand new bathroom*
- *3 bedrooms*
- *Freshly painted*
- *Vinyl plank flooring*
- *Energy efficient heating and cooling system (low bills)*
- *PET FRIENDLY*
- *LARGE fully-fenced yard*
- *Close to schools/trails/shops, etc.*

Imagine having (use profile type words for the property, i.e., your family, a businessperson like you, etc.) *in a beautiful home like this, walking out your door to the nearby* (again insert from features above, like coffee shop, trails, school) *and you living in a home where your friends and family come by and they are hit by the WOW factor of your home. This can be yours today.*

41

(If you have special offers to entice, i.e., three months Internet paid, half a month's rent first month, etc., this is where you put those)

To view and apply for this property located at (Insert full property address here so they can Google street view and/or drive by), please contact us with a phone number and email address for an application. **(Or if you have an online application (highly recommended), ask them to "click here" and include a hyperlink).**

Posting of adverts: First of all, Google the type of house and the town, for example: "3-bedroom house to rent in Surrey."

List all the places where it comes up on the first page of Google; for example, Craigslist, Kijiji, Rentboard, Rentfaster, etc. **Then post your advert in *all* of these places.**

Secondly, place them where you know locals will look, such as Facebook groups. Remember that if people Google, the search engine is *always* going to put the places that come up first in their metrics! This is why you have the home and location in the headline, the header of the body, *and* in the body itself, with the exact location. This also opens it up to people who are moving to the area and thus searching (net in-migration if you invest in a growing town, and you should be) instead of just the ones with "local knowledge." Remember that in tougher times you need every bit of help you can get to avoid vacancies, and if you do this at *all* times, good and bad, you will be more successful than others.

Keep the advert and all pictures in a file so when you know it's coming up for rent again, you can go back to the file and repost in minutes.

Photos: Again, another *highly* missed opportunity here. Take as many as you can. Most places where you post ads will let you have at least 10. Use good quality pictures (most phones are good enough, but use filters to make them better). Make sure that the picture is of the full front of the house; that the yard and driveway are clear; and that there is good lighting on the house. When taking pictures of rooms, use the "panoramic" setting. Start at one side and pan to the other. It can be a very short pano, but this way you get the whole room in a picture (and on some social media, they allow you to pan your phone and "look around." Then your pictures will typically be better than those of other people who are posting.

First picture: Front of House taken on a sunny day, no clutter on the driveway/lawn.

Second picture: Kitchen, especially if you have a nice kitchen!

Third Picture: Living room.

Fourth Picture: A feature of the house that the client will want, i.e., if it is a family, they would most likely want a nice yard for the kids. Bathroom: focus on the bathroom's positive features, like the beautiful, tiled walk-in shower with rain head, and pano from there. If it is a small bathroom, stand right at the door and pano slightly—the picture will "look" bigger than the room actually is.

Fifth/Sixth/Seventh Pictures: Bedrooms, from multiple corners/ angles (all done in pano).

Eighth Picture: Dining room.

Ninth Picture: Garage.

Tenth Picture and onwards: Other parts of the house, pano all pics, street view looking out (if it's nice), pictures of local trailheads, parks for kids, the local school, etc.

Once they respond: A tenant will fill the application and send it back to you if they are interested.

When you phone them, this will be the first time you speak to them, and you should have their application in front of you. Remember: "Sell, don't tell."

Do checks on people who pass the phone interview. Let them know that you can sign and take deposits straight away, and that they can secure the house on the spot if they want it and the showing goes well.

Show the unit to serious people for whom you have already done checks. If you meet them and they like the place, you can offer to have them sign a contract on the spot (before you show it to the next pre-qualified tenants).

Fill in the paperwork, and if they do not have the money with them, they have 24 hours to give it to you so as to keep the property. (This also prescreens the tenants for their ability to have access to money and ultimately pay your rent!)

Now you must be careful here, as *you do not want to discriminate* against anyone. For example, "suitable for…" or "no single guys" or "no one under 30" or "no kids" could be misunderstood as discrimination. When writing an advert, I would write it along the lines of:

"This wonderful family home would be a perfect place for a couple of kids to be playing in the nicely kept, fully fenced yard. There are three nice-sized bedrooms and your family can enjoy having dinner in the west-facing dining room watching the sunset over the mountains."

Notice I didn't say that a particular type of person couldn't apply, but I'm planting the seed that I'm looking for "a small family."

People reading this who are not a "small family" will most likely just pan over it, as it does not have wording they would associate with what they are looking for. In the advert, I would also put very specific instructions as I would want to see if they pay attention to detail and can follow instructions, for example:

"If you can see yourself and your family living here (plant the seed again), please email me at anyone@bestrentalsintheworldever.com, and please include the following: your full name, a phone number you can be reached at, times you are available, a little bit about you and the people who will be living here, the current area you live in, and why you think this house is suitable for you."

You want to make sure that in a sea of adverts, yours stands out. We have a sheet on our website that you can download and use as a guide: www.revnyou.com/pmbookdownloads. It will help you write an ad that will attract lots of responses from the *right* clients for your business.

Many adverts you see simply state the size, some features, the location, and the price. In our adverts, we highlight the features of the home in bullet form. (When was the last time you saw an ad for a property with the features in bulleted, "easy-to-read" format? Again, small differences can make a *huge* difference to the response rate *and* to the type of responses you get.

Step Three: Screening the Responses

If it's a family and they are moving schools mid-term, I would question why, since most parents don't move schools mid-term unless their situation is drastic! I also want to know the area they are living in currently for when I do a social media search (this is not allowed in *all* areas). Some people contact us through social

45

media when we advertise there, so I always check out as much about them as I can online. People who are serious will give you all their information. Believe it or not, I get some people that respond to the above type adverts, and all I get is an email or a private message saying *"Interested!"* Needless to say, they just prescreened themselves out of a viewing of the property.

The next stage in Step Four of prescreening is the phone call. This should be the first time you speak to them about the property. When I, or anyone at our company, talk to people on the phone, we have a set of questions we ask, tailored to each specific area. As you gain more experience, or learn harsh lessons, you will change some of the questions you ask. Again, be *very careful* not to discriminate here, and make sure your questions are general—about the person, their ability to pay the rent, and their history. During the questioning, you want to get a feeling for how they communicate. If it is difficult at this juncture, what will it be like when you need to communicate about something like late rent? We ask questions like:

1. **Why are you looking to move?**
   This should be where they give the reasons for them moving from where they are at present. What do they complain about? If it's the house, ask who the landlord is and see how they speak about him/her. Let them talk! Remember that how they talk about this current landlord is exactly how they will talk about you when they want to leave you.

2. **How much is your current rent?**
   Is this near to your rent amount? Rents go up faster in the open market than they do with a long-term tenant, so if someone suddenly had an extra $200-$500 per month in their budget based on today's market rent rate versus what they have been

paying as a long-term tenant, would their income support this? A very general rule of affordability is: salary should be minimum 3x rent.

3. **What type of home would be your ideal home?**

   Let them talk about what would be perfect for them. Their description will usually tell you what type of people they are. For example, if they want a fenced yard, family home, they probably have kids and are family-oriented. Bachelor pad, yep, probably wants a small space. If they want lots of storage, it could mean they have tons of stuff! Try to read between the lines and see how close your rental matches what they describe.

4. **Do you work, and how will you be able to afford the rent?**

   Just because someone doesn't work, that is not an indication that they cannot afford the rent. Some people get pensions, disability from work injuries, parents footing the bill, an ex-spouse paying huge child support, etc. Obviously, we prefer working people; however, some of our best tenants don't work; and some of the worst have been diligent employees, so do not let this be your only guide.

5. **Who else will be staying in the house?**

   I ask this here, and then again on the application form when they view. We have a clause in the application that states that failure to disclose any information, or providing false information, will result in one-month notice to leave. They sign to say that they accept this term on the application, so what they tell you now, should match the form.

6. **Do you volunteer anywhere?**

   This question gives us a little more information about the person. If they do volunteer, we can then verify that they do volunteer at the place they indicate, and check what they are like there as well. People who volunteer are usually more willing to give their time to help others, so it says a bit about their character.

Now this list is not exclusive or the full list we use, but a sample of questions and what they mean. When we conduct a phone interview, we also grade the answers 1, 2, or 3, with 1 being good and 3 being not so good.

For example, Q: Why are you looking to move?

A1: For a new place, something bigger (I would grade this as a 3).

A2: I'm looking to move because the house I'm in sold, so I need to find somewhere to live and I have 2 months to do so. (After verifying this as true with an MLS search, I'd grade this as a 2.)

A3: The house that we are in has sold, and I want to keep my kids in the school they are currently attending as we have four years left before they finish. Plus, my friend lives a couple of doors down, and it will be great for the kids to be close so they can play together. I like the location because it's also close to my job so I can walk to work. (I would grade this as a 1)

The lower the score, the better the candidate. Again, this is just your opinion, but use your intuition and verify all information given to you—scammers are also really good talkers!

We then have a matrix that we use, and if all the answers are low scoring and the total is below 25 (this will depend on the number of your questions), then we know we have a stronger candidate. For those who score 25-32, we investigate some of the answers further. Then 33+ scores mean that we investigate a lot further and verify information more carefully.

This helps us to remove emotion from our decision making because sometimes we feel sorry for someone and are trying to help them. However, emotional decisions are not usually a good idea when dealing with investment real estate, either with tenants or at the time of purchasing real estate, which is also when pre-screening starts. The way we set up ours is "high score, investigate more!"

Meeting the people in person

When you meet the applicants in person it will be at a set time and at the property, not before, and there are steps to follow then as well.

Viewing the property

There is a whole checklist we use (and you can have access to it) to prepare a property for viewing, so as to ensure consistency at each viewing. The checklist can be found on our website at www. rentalhouseprofits.com.

That aside, *we do not do separate viewings for each person*. We do one group viewing at two separate times, one during the *day* and one in the *evening*. If you do this, it will save you a *ton* of time. We tell the tenant a time, but we do not tell them it is a group viewing. This creates a demand and a sense of urgency for your property. Also, our time is valuable to us (and I'm sure yours is too), and the amount of last-minute cancellations and no-shows in the early days ate into our time. When the would-be tenants see 10 other people looking at the property, it ensures that they fill in their applications quickly and get them back to us. It also makes some people rule themselves out if they see others applying and they have already been unsure if they would qualify. Finally, it allows you to spend time staging the property *only once*, thus saving you time; it also means the current tenant (if there is one) has fewer interruptions; and if some people do cancel, you will still have some people who show up.

When they show up

When people do show up, it is time to be judgemental! What do they look like, dress like, and do they take care of their appearance? If they can't take care of their appearance, they are unlikely to take care of your home and future investment. What is their car like? If they are applying for a $3,000-a-month rent but are driving a wreck, I would wonder why. When they approach, do they look you in the eye? Do they offer to shake your hand? Do they have manners? All these questions go towards grading the person into groups A, B, or C, as mentioned in a previous chapter, so you can *match* them to the appropriate property.

Entering the home

When they enter the home, always have slip-on booties. If you only have one or two rentals, it may not be practicable to keep a whole box, so then let them enter first. Do they ask if they should take their shoes off, or do they take them off automatically? If they don't, ask them to take them off or to put booties on. This subconsciously tells them you are serious about keeping the property nice, but it also shows you if they are the type of person who removes their shoes! If they walk straight in without removing footwear and you have nice carpets, what will the carpets look like after 12-18 months? Again, these are not black-and-white decisions to "rent or not rent," but they are indicators of the type of people you are considering renting to. Remember—your future and how much money you end up with could be dependent on how your houses look after your investment.

Let people wander by themselves. They don't need to be told, "This is the bathroom." They can see by the fact that the toilet is there! If it is a larger home, give them a fact sheet or frequently-asked-questions sheet, such as cost of electricity, gas, and utilities based on previous tenants; any features like power in the shed, new heat pump, new windows, any upgrades, local parks, shops, schools, and any other points of interest close by. This will save you having to repeat yourself over and over.

Stay in a central point of the house—either the kitchen or the dining room—to answer any questions people may have about the application or the home. If they ask for the application, give it to them *then* and not before. Sometimes we have sent an application out beforehand and asked them to bring it to the viewing if we know them from a previous situation, but typically, we wait until they are there.

One final note: Ask people either on the phone or verbally at the viewing if they mind if you do a credit check. If they do mind, question why; if not and you have doubts about other things, then definitely run a credit check before final approval. Not every applicant goes through this, however, as we deal in properties where a lot of tenant profiles have some credit issues. Not doing checks on people who you already know *will fail* helps to keep down unnecessary costs. As a rule of thumb, however, *always* run a credit check if you are allowed to under the rules for your jurisdiction. If you do not know the applicant personally, or their references personally and *very well*, run a credit check! This can help you from getting a tenant who looks to be amazing at everything else but is financially a disaster. That scenario very rarely ends well with a rental. Depending on the market, this may not be cost effective for you. For example, lower cost housing and C tenants may have crap credit but have been paying rent as their number one priority in their lives at the expense of credit card payments. I'm okay with that!

Also, ask if they mind if you do a police check. This does one of two things: First, if they say no, this would make me question why. Or they will say, "I'll get the application to you" and just not fill it in or even come to the viewing. Or secondly, they will tell you about when they got busted in college for smoking pot or a DUI. Either way they eliminate themselves, or you get more info about who they are to help you with your decision. To be clear, we do not run police checks very often, but we use the question to elicit a response, and we use those responses to help us get a better idea of whether we want to rent to this person. Pre-screening is the point in a landlord/tenant relationship where you still have 100 percent control; do not give it away lightly.

Should I give someone a chance?

Recently I had a guy apply for a house and we asked about credit and police checks. He had been bankrupt, had his whole history printed out from Equifax, explained why it happened (divorce), and how he got it paid off, how long he had been clear, and what he was doing to ensure it didn't happen again. He had also worked for the Coast Guard for over 10 years, and he had a DUI from the police. He didn't look like an ideal tenant, given his appearance, his car, and the things mentioned above, yet he turned out to be one of our best tenants!

I personally knew his boss at the Coast Guard. It turned out that I also knew him through others as I dug for more information. So even though we screen, we screen to see how much more in-formation we need to acquire to make an educated decision, not an emotional one. If I had made an emotional or judgemental decision, I probably would not have rented to him. Screening is there to help you make educated decisions with *facts*. If you cannot acquire facts, then do not rent to them, as you are unable to make an educated decision.

You have found the perfect tenant final screening step

Once you find the perfect match for your rental, the next step is to take a *non-refundable security deposit against the first month's rent.* Try to get the whole month if possible. The reason for this is, if you take a security deposit and then they choose not to move in (which happens more often than you would think), you would have to refund the security deposit since nothing was broken, and start the process all over again.

Taking the deposit and giving them a receipt ensures that if they choose not to move in, you get to keep the money. Please note that this is legal in British Columbia, Canada—but make sure you verify local rules and regulations for your specific area. Taking the payment as soon as you agree to rent to them also shows you if they have the "spare" funds to cover a deposit as well as their current living expenses. If a tenant cannot cover this because they have to wait for the refund from their current housing provider in order to give you the deposit, this is a red flag. What happens if they have something break on their car and they do not have access to an extra $500-$2,000 (like the cost of tires!), then who are they going to *not* pay...? Yep, you guessed it—you! You want to rent to people who have money and are good with money; this will mean less headaches and it will ensure that you always get paid.

Screening tenant tips:

- Make sure the property you have suits the tenants you want.
- Write the advert for that type of tenant, highlighting what

they would like, i.e., small family=great yard, profession-al couple=walking distance to restaurants and local social events. Be careful to not discriminate against any person or type of person.

- Grade tenants to match the grade of the house.
- Have a script of questions you ask every tenant on the phone, and *always* speak on the phone before arranging a viewing.
- At viewing, verify the information they gave on the phone.
- Be judgemental when you meet, but don't be racist/sexist/ageist, or any other "ists" you can think of!
- Do the same checks on *every* tenant you think you want, even if you know them.
- Become a detective, and gather as much information as you can (as allowed by local laws) via social media, refer-ences, and credit checks. You want to know who is moving in; if you are unable to determine that, do not rent!
- Do not fall for sob stories, i.e., don't let your emotions guide you.
- Meet the tenant in person again before agreeing to rent. We usually meet at the office or for coffee to get to know them. If you allow pets, meet the pets at the viewing.
- Once you have agreed to rent to a tenant, keep in touch in the early days to deal with anything instantly until you are both satisfied. This does not mean answer every whimsical call; set the boundaries.
- Enjoy a great tenant and *business* relationship.

What if you can't screen your tenants because you inherit them with the property?

Inherited tenants – What can we do?

When you take over someone else's business, you don't get to choose the clients at the start. You will work with clients you may not like or know anything about; when you buy an already tenanted house this is what can happen.

Many people (investors) looking to buy a rental property will find a great rental that already has tenants.

Awesome! Or is it?

A few questions I would ask myself in this situation would be: Why is the current landlord selling if it's so great? Does it have something to do with the property, the landlord's life, or the tenants? So ask yourself again, if everything is great, why are they getting rid of it? There is always a reason people do something, and I would want to know why. You may never find the true answers; however, use this to help you do your due diligence before purchasing.

If there is an issue with the current tenants—refer to "screening tenant tips" above—simply ask for vacant possession (if you are allowed to) and have the seller serve notice. If you have already passed the point where the seller can issue the notice, or you need to close quickly because the seller needs out, you will have to issue the notice according to the local tenancy laws of your jurisdiction. Here in BC, we have to serve a two-month notice for the landlord's use of the property, giving them the last month's rent back, or they get the last month without having to pay rent. Either way, wherever you live, there will be a period of time where you do not have access to your unit. This can become very tricky if the tenant then decides not to move; it can become costly, time-consuming, and stressful. This is the reason I *always ask for vacant possession,* plus it gives you the ability to screen for what you want, *unless* I know the landlord and the reason he is selling, or the tenancy is new, and with amazing tenants paying current market value.

What if it's a renters' market? How hard do you screen a tenant?

In a very tight rental market, market value (rental rates) can change in a matter of a few months, if not weeks! Currently, where most of our units are located, the vacancy rate is below 1 percent. This gives you great power when screening tenants, as you have lots to choose from. Our personal vacancy rate has always been way below the market average anyway, because we provide quality rentals and screen to ensure that our clients match the property. And when you screen properly, your vacancy rate should be below the local average. If you *track* this metric, it will help you to see if your rental is "attractive" to clients, and if its not attractive, you can then assess why and improve it—but only if you track it.

If you have long-term tenants who have been fantastic with you through the steady times, then when the market goes crazy, you end up way behind by hundreds of dollars a month on those units versus market rental rates. Imagine if you inherited Mr. & Mrs. Jones, an amazing couple who have rented for nine years, have always paid rent on time, and had rent increases in line with the allowed amounts; but you're in an area with either rent control or restricted increases each year—so this rental could be way behind market rent rates. Would you want to put them out so you can raise rents to market value?

The ruthless who are reading this may be saying, "Hell, yeah!"

The super nice are going, "Ah, no, leave them there."

Me personally, I'm somewhere in the middle. I value great tenants, but as soon as a market goes crazy, you're now missing out on thousands a year. Multiply that annual thousands of dollars by the next 10 years, and you could be tens of thousands of dollars out of pocket! You are, after all, running a business! And a business is about profits, and if you are *not* about profits, then perhaps you should not be in rentals, because you could end up thousands of dollars out of pocket. If you are that "too nice person," hire a property manager who isn't!

Alternatively, when you are screening your tenants (even if you are looking to buy a place with tenants already in place), screen to see how long they are "likely" to stay there. There is an optimum for each market. In most single-family homes, three to five years is best.

You may be new to buying and managing rentals. If tenants refuse to move when you are buying a rental with people in place, usually there will have been signs of these types of people before the sale; if it's after, or either way, my recommendation would be to hire someone who is proficient at the process; use their skills and pay them for it. The savings in your sanity and time will be worth every penny you spend on this. I have a few local Realtors who ask me to do this for them from time to time. When a tenant realizes that you know the tenant laws and are not being taken in by their "poor-me" stories, *and that you can work together to reach to a solution*, you will usually get a much quicker resolution to the problem. And *all of this* can be avoided if you use good screening techniques with the tenants even before you buy or put an offer on the property.

Top tips when buying a house with tenants already in place:

For owner's personal use (for real):

- Ask the seller to provide vacant possession on closing. This may make the close date further away but it is definitely worth the wait.

- If unable to wait, serve notice the day you get possession. Do not delay. Offer to compensate the tenant for leaving early—you just paid hundreds of thousands for a house; what is a couple thousand extra to actually have it? Maybe even get half from the seller!
- Ensure all steps are followed to the letter of the local rules and regulations.

If keeping tenants:
- Make sure all paperwork is accounted for, and if not, have them fill out new paperwork. Ask to see receipts or proof of payment for rent, deposits etc. If no contracts are in place to verify rental amounts, do not just ask them—verify everything.
- Complete a full application so you know who your new tenants are, and you know how to deal with them moving forward.
- When was the rent last raised? Can you increase it now? Do you want to?
- What are your options in case these people do not work out?
- Inspect the home thoroughly before purchase, and again as soon as the purchase is completed to make sure it is exactly how it was at the building inspection. Ensure that you did not miss anything on your walk through.

Selecting appropriate tenants can be the difference between success and failure in your business. It can be the difference between keeping your sanity or going crazy. Screening is your last line of defence against bad tenants. Get this right and 90 percent of your headaches will be resolved!

CHAPTER 5

HANDING OVER THE KEYS TO YOUR CASTLE–MOVE-IN AND INSPECTION

This is it—you are about to give the keys to your $300,000-$500,000–dollar investment to someone who is potentially a stranger. You are happy to have found someone to pay your bills, yet apprehensive because do you "really" know them? Well, if you did the things in the previous chapter on screening, you should be pretty confident. Now it is about ensuring your processes of execution are in order, and that is where this chapter will help you.

All references have checked out, deposits have been paid and cleared in the accounts, and it's move-in day. NUMBER 1 RULE: do not allow anyone to cross the threshold unless all monies have been paid *and* you have done the walk-around and move-in inspection and paperwork. When doing the inspection, use the government forms issued by your local Tenancy Branch or another approved professional group, and add to them by taking pictures. When you take pictures, also make sure you snap a couple with the *tenant* in the picture so they cannot say they were not present during the inspection.

Prior to this, before they arrive, go around and set up the house, making sure the temperature is correct, the lights are all on, and fresh air has passed through. Basically, it is very similar to the checklist we use before showing a property to potential tenants (available at www.rentalhouseprofits.com). Also take a video of the home, and if you see any marks or wear-and-tear, record them on the move-in inspection form. Allow a good 30 minutes to do this inspection.

Do your inspections *before* the tenant arrives so you are aware of any deficiencies. You also want to make sure you test each electrical outlet. You can buy a socket tester for about $30 that lights up when it is wired and working correctly. Check each switch for operation; check all the blinds and curtains to make sure they work; and check in the corners of all closets, drawers and cupboards. Use a small flashlight for the dark corners and a small stepladder if you can't see above things.

You want to check all of these because the tenant—your new client—is most likely going to look for faults as they walk around, or at best find them as they start living there. A technique I use to stop myself from missing things or brushing them aside, is to make a game out of it, since we all view the world, including our own rentals, through rose-tinted glasses. For every item on the checklist that I find, I give myself $2. Why would I do this? Well, it makes me look harder, but it also rewards me for being thorough, and if I raise enough money from the process, I treat myself with the money—a muffin from the coffee shop, a cup of tea, or in some cases a whole lunch!

What I'm doing (and what you will do if you adopt the same strategy) is teaching my brain and subconscious to look for things like a tenant would when they move in. This ensures that you either get the things resolved before the tenant moves in, or make a note so it can be pointed out to the tenant and then you can agree on a suitable time to fix it. Then you don't suddenly have the rose-tinted glasses off when the tenant moves out and suddenly have the eyes of a hawk because you do not want to refund them! This can save your sanity, prevent confrontations, and ultimately be less stress for you. We as rental housing providers typically look over faults on move-in because we *want* the tenant; and we scrutinize more for faults when they move out because we *want* to keep the deposit! You should *love* giving deposits back—it's the best! It means they looked after your investment and were an awesome client!

Once the tenants arrive at the house, remove your shoes, setting an example so they know what to expect. Again, all of these little things feed the subconscious mind of the tenant. You can then slowly go through each room, and point out everything you have added to the form and each line highlighting all things in good condition. There are forms on the Tenancy Branch websites to help you check each room. I have seen people put a line though the whole lot and then write, "okay." Not sure how this would stand up in court if you needed to make a claim, so do things fully and thoroughly. It's always better to be over-the-top than not thorough enough. At the end of the day, it's your money you'll be losing if things are not done correctly.

Remember when you moved in a new house? Was it a pleasant experience or was there some stress involved? Most likely the latter. Be aware that this is probably the same for the people moving into your rental home, which they are about to pay you handsomely for. Being armed with this knowledge, try to ensure that even though you want to be very thorough, their time is valuable. Now is *not* the time to engage in long conversations about anything other than the inspection. Make sure to show your new tenants where all emergency items are, like the water shut-off and electrical panels, and then arrange to come back either the next day or the day after at the very latest. Why? Well, you want to make sure they are settling in and you want to see if they have any issues so you can deal with them straight away.

Before they leave, hand over the keys and a welcome basket, in which you can put a "congratulations on your new home" card, as well as things they might need straight-away, like a couple of rolls of toilet paper and some dish soap. Usually we put some nice chocolates and a coffee shop card in there, and the basket is worth around $30. How many landlords do you know do this? Probably none or very few. This differentiates you from the crowd, makes you out to be a decent guy or girl, and helps to start building a good working relationship with your new client. Tenants do not get welcome baskets, but clients do! Some things you can put into your welcome basket/bag include:

- A "welcome to your new home" card, hand signed, in blue ink
- Chocolates
- Baked goods, cookies, breads, etc. Homemade is good if you can make nice things; I buy mine.
- Coffee shop gift cards
- Toilet rolls
- Wet wipes
- Dish soap
- A scratch card from the lottery (usually they have a "new home" one).
- Any other little thing that makes people smile

Note: We have a checklist of all the things to take with you, and all the steps to take to ensure your walkthroughs are thorough

*and consistent. You can make your own, or you can visit www.
rentalhouseprofits.com/shop where we have a ton of premade lists to
help you and save you a lot of time. They cost less than a cheap cup of
coffee and you can pick and choose the ones you need.*

When you return the next day (or the day after), bring copies
of the tenancy agreement they signed, and copies of the move-in
inspection and the tenant handout folder. (More on this folder later.) Now is the time to have a longer conversation about the property, and to go over expectations for lawns and maintenance and
anything else they are responsible for. All of this should also be in
the tenant handout folder you give them. At this time, also say
that you forgot to test the electrical outlets in the bedrooms with
your tester. This allows you to go into the house to see how things
are after they have moved stuff. For example, if you are renting to
a family of four, but there are eight beds, I would question that in
my head and monitor!

I like to have a conversation with the tenant(s) so I can get to
know a bit more about them and gather details that will help me
provide a better service. Are they old or busy and would therefore
like to use your "lawn guy or girl"? Having, or knowing about,
other complimentary services will show that you care about them
and your property. You want to be friendly but not friends; keep
it business. You can discuss interesting things about the area like
where the good hikes are, or what noted things of interest are
around to see and do. This will both engage them in conversation
and offer you more insight into who they are. And it will offer
them added value regarding the home they have chosen and why
living in your rental and area rocks!

We also go through *The Tenant Handout Folder*, which they sign,
and they promise to pay a $70 fee to replace it if it's lost or dam-

aged. This is done to add an air of importance to the folder you are about to hand them. You will have briefly gone through the contents of that folder when they initially moved in; but now, add the inspection forms and the copies of the agreements, and go a little more into depth about each item.

This folder serves several purposes: It ensures that they understand the property and what needs to be done; what constitutes an emergency and how to contact the correct people in case of one; and how to submit maintenance requests with a clear description so we can forward it to our trades and they will know what is needed. It also includes all of their new resident information, a welcome letter laying out our expectations of the tenancy, monthly inspection rules and requirements, and common things they will need to deal with in the house. For example: if there are aluminum windows and they live in BC, there's a good chance they'll get mildew and mold on them. Many people do not realize it is the tenant's responsibility to keep these windows clean, so we include "how to" guides for doing so, along with a Tenancy Act section that explains that it is their responsibility.

You want to ensure that everything you place in the tenant hand-out folder helps prevent any misunderstandings, explaining clearly who is responsible for what, with the evidence to show why, i.e., excerpts from the Tenancy Act. You want to ensure that the folder has appropriate things specifically for the area where you rent—winterizing, parking rules, by-laws, whatever is going to help them be hassle-free clients for you.

Probably one of the first items you want to include are the move-out rules and procedures. In very clear formatting, and concisely explaining the consequences, tell your clients the processes you want them to follow and what will happen if they don't. We have these available on our website www.rentalhouseprofits.com and if you go to the website and put in the code that we give you later in the book, you can have access to these for free. We explain that if they need to move out before the contract ends—if they signed a long-term lease, for example—we will work with them to find a new tenant so they have no liability upon leaving. Usually we get two to three months' notice if someone is going to leave and break a lease, which gives us plenty of time to plan, advertise, and screen new replacements. This helps to reduce vacancy and saves time and money again and again. When you start doing this on your rentals, you will see a big shift in how they interact with you at the end. Here is an example of what usually happens in most cases, and why it is important to discuss move-out procedures when the renter is just moving in.

You may or may not have given proper instructions to your client about move-out and breaking the lease, but in any case, you'll be following the laws in your jurisdiction. In British Columbia, where we operate, here's what would happen:

October 31, you'd receive notice of the tenant intending to vacate on November 30.

You begin advertising on November 1.

You begin showing the property a few days later (if you can coordinate the times with your current tenants and have them get the place looking show ready).

By November 7 you will have applicants to go through and screen.

By November 9 you will probably have completed the reference checks and selected your tenant, but they then need to give their current landlord 30 days notice, so now you are not going to have anybody in the property on December 1; you have to wait until January 1!

Giving people the move-out procedures, and letting them know that if they break the lease early you will work with them to help find new clients and reduce their liability, it shifts from the scenario above to one where they give you two or three months' notice, thus allowing you to have fewer vacancies and ultimately putting more money in your pocket.

You can create your own folder, or again, you can download ours for less than the price of a couple of cups of coffee at *www.revnyou. com/shop* and then grow yours from that. The point is to communicate things to your tenant in a clear way that helps you both understand how the relationship needs to work and what systems to follow to get the best results.

Once a new tenant moves in, speak to *all* the neighbours, who by the way always have your number and cards so they can call you if needed. This helps put the neighbours at ease when you are able to explain who your new tenant is, and to remind them that if there are ever any issues, they can contact you and you will deal with them immediately. This ensures that you have a free security team watching your house! It also prevents the neighbours from ever getting into a conflict with your tenants. If you are an active real estate investor and rental house purchaser, this can also show the neighbours you are a professional and that you actually care—they may even become clients of yours in the future, as tenants or investors! As an example of how valuable this process is: We did this at a rental and the owner across the alley came over and spoke to us about rentals. After a few conversations about our rental and his, he offered us his property at a reasonable price: $160,000. We bought it,

spent about $40,000 to fix it up, and a year later it was worth $350,000—a $150,000 profit! A simple process netted us a huge return. It's a process we do when every tenant moves in, and you can see how valuable it is!

CHAPTER 6

COMMUNICATE WITH *YOUR* MONEY

If you gave a total stranger, who filled in a questionnaire and had a couple of references, $300,000 cash in a bag and asked them to look after it, how often would you contact them to see if the money was okay? How much of an interest would you take in their life? Would you make sure you had their correct phone number? Now ask yourself—when was the last time you communicated with you tenant? I know this seems like a silly metaphor, yet this is how I view my rental units—as bags of cash that are going to pay for my present and future goals and dreams, whether that will be college for kids, holidays, retirement, or travel.

Now communication needs to be just that—communication, and not a one-way transmission. How many of you can say that the only time you speak to your tenant is when it's time to collect rent, or questioning them if the rent is late, or when something needs to be fixed? For many owners, this is the *only* time they speak to their tenants. In my opinion, this creates a negative relationship, one in which every time you see their number on your phone, you feel yourself sink inside and you wonder: "What now?" Imagine them now as clients who spend thousands in your business. Would you send them thank you cards or rewards, or speak to them occasionally to see how things are? This way, they will see your name on a phone text or email and not immediately have a sinking feeling that something must be wrong!

We have a standard policy with our tenants—that in order to rent one of our properties, we are connected with them on social media. We cannot enforce this due to privacy laws, but if someone didn't want to connect, I would question why in my mind. Yep, they get to see what's happening in my life, and I get to see what is happening in theirs. This may seem crazy, but how many of you are connected through social media to people you hardly know? I bet if you went through your social media, most of you would not be able to tell me, by looking at the names, where you met them all, and how you know them. So why then would a person not want to share their social profile with someone who shares a vested interest in a $300,000-$800,000 home? They wouldn't! Unless they had something to hide.... Perhaps it's a case of going around once a month to do a check-up, where they can let you know what's up with the property (if anything). That might be another way you could connect; however, in today's world, social media is the easiest way to communicate and stay connected. If you are not willing to connect and share, you are missing a big potential opportunity to communicate with your clients.

Now if you have 1,000+ properties, you might want to start a Facebook page or group instead of using your personal profile; but if you are like me, and have under 100 rental properties (currently), your personal profile is a great resource. And it is amazing what information people will relay through social media that they would not say to you in person. This also lets you know who is looking after your future, and it typically shows you pictures of how it is being looked after. Like the time I saw online that a tenant had posted pictures showing that her dog had just had puppies and they had wrecked the house! She would never have told me that face-to-face, but I was able to screenshot it and add it to the folder that we keep regarding our tenants. This was important in case it wasn't all repaired, and we therefore would need to file a claim. (And by the way, we did have to file a claim. It's also good for when you get the inevitable sob stories that rent will be late due to "blah, blah, blah, and therefore lack of funds." Yet online, they were at a concert, bought a new car, and got a tattoo (true story). Being connected to your tenants online helps you make educated decisions and *not* emotional ones. We use social media to communicate with our tenants, and Facebook, being the one most people currently use, also allows you to see when they received messages and when they read them, which is great for holding them accountable to responding, and if they're not responding, it means you need to investigate.

We also periodically pop 'round and do things like clean the windows and gutters as well as other tasks that make their home nicer. That way, they can see we take pride in our property. We also ensure that they feel comfortable talking to us about what is going on in their lives, and we do this by developing our skills as a listener! Remember: "two ears, one mouth." So, when you are around your clients, it's about *them*, not you. It is still business for you! This also helps to build trust in the relationship, so that if and when things get a bit negative, because that is life (and the profile of our tenants where we invest), we can usually work with them to provide solutions around the rental. While some communication is inevitably going to be negative, there are many opportunities to make it positive. You can congratulate your tenants on their accomplishments; you can say "happy birthday" and send them birthday cards; and you can send them cards at various festive times of the year. This makes them more loyal than if you only communicate when something goes wrong.

DISCLAIMER: *We do not allow emotions to rule these decisions. We will work with a tenant who may be going through a tough patch in life, yet we still issue all paperwork and notices as if we were going to evict. Then even if we don't, we have all the necessary things if the situation ever escalated or got worse.*

Having good communication with your tenants—which means you can talk to them, you know what is happening in their life (as best as you can), and they want to actually speak to you—helps you to make more educated decisions when, for example, someone has been fantastic for one or two years and then goes through a breakup, job loss, or other life event. We will be more lenient and help them figure out a solution if they have communicated what has been happening, versus not hearing anything and then suddenly we hear, "Sorry, the rent is going to be late." However, if the situation continues, we will issue an eviction and follow through, regardless of what is happening. We care about our tenants, but we also care about ourselves, our investors, our homeowners, and their families.

The way you speak and the actions you take should is something you must consider when you are on the property. Simple things like when you walk up the drive or past the yard and see a piece of litter, pick it up and place it in the garbage. This sets an example of what you want them to do; and do this whether you see them or not—you never know if they are watching. If you engage in conversation with them and you are discussing the property, be very careful to use positive influencers such as, "Wow, the yard looks amazing now that the grass has been cut!" or "Great job on (insert any job they have done well)!" If they do something over and above what is expected—one guy built a storage unit in the back garden for tools—go and get them something as a reward.

Not all communication will be positive, though, as we have seen. When things go wrong or break, which they will, get the situation resolved as soon as possible. *After* it has been resolved, offer something to the tenant—this could be a gift card for the coffee shop they use, or in severe cases where a pipe burst or something drastic like that, offer some money off rent that month to make up for the hassle that was not their fault. What this does is show them you care about *them*; not just their money.

Here are some rules you should always follow *whenever* you communicate with a tenant: it ensures good communication practices, which will result in a better rental housing provider/client relationship.

- Never communicate when you are angry.
- Never communicate anything that can be used against you at a hearing.
- Never communicate a response without thinking for at least five minutes.
- Never EVER allow them to swear or shout at you—set behavior boundaries and stick to them.
- Never EVER raise your voice or swear at a tenant. If you feel things escalating, simply say that you will come back when everyone is calm. Then walk away!
- Never EVER blame—because they will then become defensive. Look for solutions to the problem. And after it's been resolved, figure out why it happened, so you can prevent it from happening again.
- Never EVER be the *top* of the ladder. I always have a higher authority I have to verify things with, so if a tenant asks

me something and I don't agree, I can say that I have to check with [insert name here]. Then if the answer is not favorable to them, you can say, "I asked and they said no. Sorry, I tried." This puts you on their side and things don't become confrontational!

- Always record conversations you have with your tenant on the phone (In B.C., you do not need to tell them you are recording.) Your tenant may become angry, and having a recording could save your bacon if they end up going to the police or you have to use it in a hearing (see story below).

- Always have a solution *before* contacting the tenant, so you can let them know what is possible for you to do.

- Always keep track of *all* communication—even if it's friendly. We record our conversations in outline form and save them in the tenant file with date/time/topic.

- Always respond as soon as is practicably possible. If I'm out with friends, for example, I send a text with a time that I will contact them, as I am available, unless it is an emergency—a real one.

- Always use the correct paperwork. Always.

- Always give them a letter explaining in amicable terms why certain paperwork is being given, and offer solutions within the paperwork. We do this even with 10-day eviction notices.

This list is not exclusive, but it's a good start for things to do and not to do.

The lying woman story

Once upon a time we were going to communicate with a difficult person we had inherited as part of our property management

74

company. I had to go to the tenant's door and I feared it would be confrontational due to the other person's nature and the issue at hand. I put my phone on video record and knocked on the door. She came to the door, and despite my staying totally calm, communicating the necessary information, and being polite and courteous, she escalated the conversation and started spouting a load of lies. I handed her the paperwork I wanted to deliver and she slammed the door in my face.

I left the house and thought nothing of it until I received a call from the police asking me to come to the station. The only reason they did that, instead of coming down to arrest me, was because the officer knew me and figured it was unlikely I had behaved in the way she claimed. Otherwise I would have been in handcuffs!

So, I went down to the station, where the officer informed me that my tenant had said she was afraid of me because I banged on her door and when she answered I started threatening her. She also said that because I had a black eye (which I had received from playing soccer four days earlier), she figured that I was a violent person and she feared for her safety. I laughed at this whole charade, and when the officer asked me for my side of things, I said, "I have a video."

When I showed it to him, he was shocked at how different the reality was from her story. He apologized to me and asked if I would send him a copy. Then he went back to the woman and cautioned her about wasting police time and engaging in slander.

If this had gone to a hearing, that recording would have played in my favor. So, protect yourself, keep records, and *never* put anything in a text or email, or a format that could be used against you should things escalate. I don't want to scare you into thinking that most people are bad or difficult, and some of these examples are the exception to the norm; but the exception could be the very thing that puts you off having an amazing financial future with real estate if you do not deal with things correctly.

Communications management

Good management can prevent a lot of negative things from happening; but if you are in the game long enough, you will encounter some negative things. Too often people buy a house, find a tenant, put them into the unit, and then have no contact with them as long as the rent is coming in—and this could be for a year or even longer. Then the owner goes to the unit after the tenancy ends and is shocked by the condition of the house.

This type of experience can even end people's dream of real estate investing, and they sell the house, sometimes at a discount, just to be free from the hassle. When I hear these stories, I feel sorry for them, because this can be avoided a lot of the time—either by them managing differently, or by them getting *a good property manager* who can manage it for them, and usually for very little in the big scheme of things. Having good communication practices will help prevent a lot of negative things from escalating.

Imagine if you pay your property manager $1,500-$2,000 a year but the mortgage paydown is $10,000+ or the property appreciation is $15,000+ per year. You as the business owner "give away" a potential $25,000-30,000 a year because you failed to manage correctly or were too cheap to use a professional to help you. It seems silly when you put it down on paper, yet I see this repeatedly. Or after one bad incident that was just unlucky, the buyer gives up and never invests in property again.

Imagine going out for a meal, and you get an unpleasant meal or even food poisoning, so you never go out for another meal *ever!*

So, you miss out on all the benefits of those experiences because you allow one or two bad incidents to ruin your future. If you are sitting there and saying: I have had *way more* than two bad incidents with my properties, there are two things it could be. Either you have a lot of properties and understand it is part of the game, or you need to learn how to manage and communicate better and/or get someone to manage for you.

Systems and processes

Management can be broken down into systems and processes. It's easier to manage people when you have systems and processes in place that you can monitor and improve upon. If you aren't getting the results you want, then modify the systems and processes. We have checklists for everything we can think of when it comes to the management of our properties—from screening tenants, to setting up the viewing, to the checklists we give to the cleaning companies—yes, we give checklists to the cleaners, the trades guys, the handymen, and anyone else who works for us. We give them checklists for the work and have them sign off on each item. This way we can ensure consistency in every field, and accountability if it's not done. It also ensures that they know what we want done and how we want it done.

Creating your own checklists is awesome for another reason too: it will make you think through each step of the various processes. When we first started, we had checklists for the things we did the most, or the things where we had different people doing the same tasks, like different cleaning companies. We did all of this so we could start to get consistency across the results, and it also allowed us to compare apples to apples when paying for services.

Here is a copy of our monthly inspection checklist. As you can see, it does not matter who does it, because they will have the same process and a sign-off for accountability.

Checklist 5A monthly Checklist

Although we are allowed to do monthly inspections, we do not recommend annoying "good" tenants with this, again depending on property tenant profile, etc. We recommend doing one a month after they move in, and then, depending on the condition at this point, we wait two months after that. Then if it's still great, we do bi-annual *full* inspections. We still do *monthly* drive-by inspections of the house, where we get out, check the yard, look at the gutters, etc., and if any issues are there, we arrange to speak to the tenant. We explain that our inspections are a requirement of our maintenance, insurance, and accident prevention (from leaks and such).

Before conducting an inspection:

- Give the correct written form for 24 hours notice to enter the property, and ideally hand it to the tenant rather than leaving it on the door. (If it is served on the door, you may have to wait longer to enter.)
- Have a copy of the last inspection, and if none, a copy of the move-in inspection report.
- Ensure you have the following: camera, nitrile gloves, boot covers, pens, basic tools, screwdriver, screws, hammer, plug-in electrical socket tester.
- Have the inspection reporting form.

At inspection:

◊ When entering the property, place boot covers over your shoes.

◊ Inspect the following:
- All sink drains. Fill and then pull plug, and check un-

derneath for leaks from pipes.
- All electrical outlets using electrical tester.
- All blinds for full operation.
- All windows that open for operation.
- Visual inspection behind all doors for damage to walls.
- Behind fridge and stove for cleaning.
- All locks on all doors for functionality.
- Dryer for operation, any squeaks, etc.
- Washing machine: check the hoses behind and the drain for signs of leaking.

Back at office: (check box when complete)
◊ Make a copy to return to tenant after three days—with pass or with remedial work that needs to be done (by you or by them).
◊ File in tenant folder to keep as record.

Preparation list of things to take:
- Keys to property
- Plug in electrical socket tester
- Pens
- Camera (if your phone doesn't have one)
- Boot covers
- Basic tool kit, i.e., Philips screwdriver, small flathead, #2 Robertson, small hammer, small crescent wrench.

Checklist completed by:

_____ print & sign

Notes:

Even if you use a professional management company, you can use your own checklists to make sure they use your standards. Again, we have A LOT of checklists for all the things we do, and we have them online at *www.revnyou.com/shop*

Checklists save you money

Checklists are also good to have in a "what-if" scenario. We classify "what-ifs" as anything that might happen but mostly won't. For example, what if one of your tenants dies on the property? For this, I would have a "what-if" you are informed about it, and a "what-if" you find the body. Could this happen? Probably…people die every day. Are they likely to die in the house? Less likely, but it could happen. Fair chance they are not paying rent if they die, so what's the procedure? Do you have next of kin on their application form anywhere? Do you know the steps to get possession of the property?

Typically, if you are searching when it happens, you will be more emotional, and we all know emotional decisions are less thought out than practical, educated ones. What-if someone just stopped paying rent? If you have a checklist to follow, even though you feel emotional—stressed, angry, upset, or any of the other emotions that cloud our judgment—you just follow the steps. This will help you to become less stressed, help you focus on the solution and not the problem, and finally help save your sanity and prevent you from overreacting. This alone can save you thousands of dollars in making unnecessary, incorrect actions.

The more reactive you are to situations, the more stress you will create in your life! Having systems and processes in place to address any situation will reduce stress, save your sanity, and stop money going down the drain and being wasted.

Good management allows you to plan ahead, foreseeing problems before they become problems and alleviating unwanted stress and expense from your investment. Good checklists help with communication between you and your tenant, and also allow you to prevent a lot of reactive situations, again reducing stress in your real estate business.

What about when you have followed every step we've covered so far and the tenant becomes difficult or refuses to move? Some people, for whatever reason, will become difficult. Remember, if this happens, that it is not about *you*; do not take anything personally. They obviously have other things going on in their life that you may or may not be aware of, and nor is it any of your business. Understand that even if it seems like there is no end to what is happening, there is always a solution, and your systems and processes will show you that path. Regardless of whether we "feel" (see emotion creeping in) what's happening is right or wrong, there will be a clear path to follow, and it must be followed to resolve the issue at hand. Bad situations usually come from bad management. Not always, but if we are grown up about things, we will be able to see where **we made a mistake** that contributed to the situation.

If a tenant is not paying, it's possible that you did not select the right tenant originally. Unfortunately, we have nearly always contributed either directly or indirectly to what appears in our life. This can come from a lack of knowledge or a lack of experience, and I can say this because I have been at fault for all of the hard lessons I have learned in real estate. What I ask myself after each mistake or experience is: **WHAT CAN I DO TO ENSURE THIS DOES NOT HAPPEN AGAIN?**

Addendums: A great way to communicate your wishes to the new tenant client, without having to verbally tell them what you want and what you do not want, is to add a great set of addendums to the rental contract.

If you have a rental contract and do not have any addendums, I would highly recommend you change your strategy and include some. These are a way not only to clarify things, but also to strengthen your position if you ever need to go to a hearing to get your property back or evict a tenant. A good set of addendums also helps you manage your tenant because you *both* have the addendum to refer to regarding what needs to be done, rather than you having to tell them. Addendums, when written correctly, are also a way to help you navigate the tricky waters of some of the rules of the Act or regulations that may be hindering your effective management.

For example, here in BC, we are prevented from raising rents by more than the amount the government dictates. We cannot fine a tenant if they are late paying rent, even if it takes a lot of time to deal with the situation. Also, at the end of a term contract, say one year, we can only revert to a month-to-month, which can be a problem for a landlord when you want to borrow money for other projects or grow your portfolio, and rental rates are below market value—lenders typically ask for one-year contracts, and my insurance asks for one-year contracts too. To get around this, we have an addendum that states:

If the rent is paid on time, a $200 instant rebate of rent will be applied and only $xxxx will be paid. Failure to pay on time without written notice from the landlord or property manager will result in the rent reverting back to the original amount of $xxxx. This instant rebate reduction is only for one-year contracts and above; if your contract is expiring or reverting to a month-to-month, you can contact your property manager or *landlord to extend the contract, thus enabling the rebate to remain in force. This rebate is at the discretion of the property manager and landlord, and it can be removed or reduced at any time if all the terms of the rental agreement are not fully met.*

This does a few things: it ensures the tenant will pay their rent on time or pay an extra $200. If they are going to be late, they contact you well in advance to avoid paying the extra money. To date, I have not had to enforce this $200 rule, because if they give me plenty of notice and a solution, then I am okay and usually more lenient. If someone is repeatedly late and it becomes a hassle, they can pay the $200 extra every month, which equals $2,400 a year. Is that worth the hassle of chasing them? Your decision. It also ensures that now the tenant has a vested interest in making sure their contracts are one year long and that they keep renewing, giving power back to the landlord in this case. To clarify, I do not reduce rent to below market. I advertise say, $1,200 a month (market rent, and what they will pay if they pay on time), and then on the contract, I write $1,400 (above market rent by $200) and *then* give them the monthly discount. This gives them an incentive to make sure they pay on time as well!

The regulations in BC state that after a year, rent reverts to a monthly contract unless the tenant agrees on an extension. Before, they had no reason to renew the contract dates, which would reduce their liability to you if they just up and left, but now it gives power back to the landlord in that same situation. Also, if rent controls in your area do not allow rental increases aligned with the market, you have the ability, as it is at your discretion, to reduce the rebate amount so you are not increasing rent, but reducing the *rebate amount.* You still get more money in your pocket but you do not break the rules. If you are in an area where this rule applies, or looks like it may happen in the future, I would set my tenancy agreements higher with a bigger rebate that could be removed if need be. I am presently making my rebate $300 to alleviate any future controls our current provincial government is looking at to screw over landlords—I mean to help generate more affordable housing for tenants. If your tenant always pays on time, you can send a letter showing them how much they have saved by paying on time: $300 per month=$3,600 per year. Send a letter congratulating them and put a thank you card with a gift card in it. Make yourself different and better than others!

Here is a list of current addendums I use for the market and the types of homes I currently invest in. These will vary based on the types of people you have, the properties, and the local regulations, so you may need to adjust slightly to comply and to suit your purposes. Remember, the worst that can happen is that an adjudicator in court might say that something is not allowed—that doesn't mean it hasn't had the desired effect on the previous 20 tenants that signed it!

Addendum to rental contract:
Sign bottom of page 1 & 2 to confirm you agree and have read and understand them.

1. Any damage incurred to the property by the tenant, the tenant's pets, or visitors of the tenants will be charged back to the tenant on a per incident basis. Failure to pay for said damages as they occur will be considered a breach of contract and the tenants will have one month's notice to vacate the property.
   Theoretically they could cause damage and not repair it until they moved out. This allows you to charge and potentially evict if they do not repair things immediately.

2. All our properties are NO SMOKING of any materials, including cigarettes, e-cigarettes, marijuana even if for medical. Damage caused by smoking in the property or on the property will remain the liability of the tenant, and on completion of this contract, any expenses incurred for cleaning, repainting, or any other such matter associated in any way with the smoking, will be charged to the tenant and you accept this responsibility. Any evidence of smoking will result in one month's notice to vacate the property and you accept this term.

   We do not allow smoking in the units and this gives you/us the power to enforce that. If we find they have smoked during the tenancy, we use an ozonator (see useful references at the end of this book) in the property for 24-48 hours. This removes the smoke from the walls and flooring. Note that you cannot be in the property when this is being done.

3. It will remain the responsibility of the tenant to clear driveways and adjoining pathways in front of the home of snow and also any debris that may block the driveways and pathways.

   I live in Canada. It snows sometimes. If people are unable to do this, we can increase the rent by xx per month and hire it out. Collect the amount for the season spread out into payments over the year and add it to the rent—do not take away from your rent and cash flow.

4. The yard is to be kept clean as much as possible from any mess associated with any animals whether owned by the tenant or not. If this is not adhered to, a **$50 fee** will be imposed on each incident when the landlord comes around and sees any evidence. Repeated offences will be considered a breach of contract, and the tenant agrees to one month's notice to vacate the property.

We are pretty strict on this one—too often people have left and if they had pets, which most of ours do, the last thing on their mind is to clean up their dog's mess, especially if it's winter. The issue may never arise until spring, long after they have gone, so consider a retainer if that is the case.

5. In the circumstance that an NSF charge or check bounce fee or late payment occurs, there will be an administration cost of **$75.** This is not a fine and it is to cover *the cost of time* required to deal with this circumstance and the NSF fee charged by our bank.

   Again, NOT A FINE but an expense to be covered for the time required to deal with this. If you can charge a fine, go for it and ask for as much as you can get away with, but basically this should be a deterrent, not an income generator.

6. If any other adults move into the premises for longer than 3 (three) nights, or for more than 14 nights in total over the course of a year, then written notice must be given to the landlord. Failure to do so will be a breach of contract and will be considered as one month's notice to vacate the property. If another person moves into the property and this is agreed to by the landlord or property manager, then rent will increase by $100 per month. This is for extra wear and tear on the property.

   We are okay with people having visitors for a week or two, like family; this clause is to prevent them moving people in randomly and using the property as a glorified hotel. It is also meant to deter one person from applying who is awesome but then you find out their grandson or nephew, who may not have been approved, is also living there. This gives you some power to evict non-contracted individuals.

7. As a tenant you will be responsible for keeping lawns and gardens associated with the property in good condition, and

also up to a standard that is in keeping with the neighbour-hood. This means lawns mowed, hedges trimmed, leaves cleared up in fall, and all other grounds work associated with the property. Failure to do so will mean that Rental House Profits will hire professionals to do so, and the cost incurred will be charged back to the tenant on a per inci-dent basis. Failure to pay will be considered by both parties as a breach of contract and there will be one month's notice to vacate the property.

We offer the option of either a small rent increase or having our company cut their lawns all year. This spreads out the cost and ensures it is always done to our satisfaction. It also gives us the power to ensure that our tenants look after the property and it gives them a sense of pride in looking after it.

8. If you are entered into our rent reduction program, paying rent on time will result in a *$200 rent reduction program*, and the instant rebate will be applied to your monthly amount so only $_____ will have to be paid. This will remain in effect as long as your rent is paid on time and subject to the discretion of the property manager. If your rent is late, then the rent will revert back to the original contract amount of $_____ This rebate is only in force with one-year term contracts; then on expiry of the term, a new term must be agreed to for the rebate to remain in place. This rebate is at the discretion of the property manager and landlord and can be removed at any time if ALL of the terms of the rental contract are not fully met. You are signing to agree to this term.

9. As a tenant, **you must obtain tenant content insurance to cover the cost of your belongings, and tenant liability insurance for a minimum of $1,000,000 liability**, sign to

say you have read and agreed to this statement, and show us the insurance certificate. This is to be completed before keys are issued, and failure to do so may result in ending the tenancy early. You accept this term.

There are many reasons you want the tenant to have insurance—it saves you money in potential deductible, and it provides them with protection if anything happens to the property and/or their belongings. Also, your insurance could be void if they do not have insurance for certain things, so it is always good to make sure your policy covers everything and theirs too. Read all your insurance before you need to.

10. You are responsible for ensuring the property is locked at all times when vacant, and failure to do so will incur a fine of $100. Also, the cost of any damage incurred through the neglect of the tenant leaving the door unlocked will be charged back to the tenant on a per incident basis. You are signing this and agree to pay any costs for this if they arise.

    Doors left open allow people to walk in and break or steal things...if you did not add this, YOUR INSURANCE would be paying. That way, they are liable for repairs and the cost of damages.

11. You are responsible for the keys for your property, and if any keys are lost, the locks will be changed. As the tenant, you agree to pay for the lock change. The charge for this is $300, and failure to pay will result in a breach of contract and deemed as one month's notice to vacate the property. Only our approved locksmiths may be used to repair and replace locks at any time. You accept this term upon signing.

    This gives you some power over what is done to YOUR property. People often fix things with the cheapest possible solutions when you may have spent hundreds on top quality security locks.

12. You must sign the tenant handout folder and initial this form to verify that you have read and fully understand all of the items in the addendum and in the tenant handout folder. This folder must be returned on completion of the tenancy, and failure to do so will result in a charge of $75 dollars. This is for the time and cost to replace the folder.

    This charge helps to create a value to the folder that you give them, and ensures that they look after it. If they do not, it pays for your time to make another one.

13. "If no pet deposit is paid, no pets are allowed on the premises. This means no friends or family with pets are allowed to visit and no pet-sitting is allowed." Tenant has read and agreed to this statement.

    This prevents people from saying they have no pets, and then after moving in, there is always this dog or cat around. We had a guy who told us he was pet-sitting and when we checked his Facebook, the last two months of profile pictures were of him and the dog. In fact, he had changed his profile picture to the dog! Not normal behavior if you have a friend dropping their pet off for a few hours. Needless to say, the revelation helped us create this addendum! So, thank you.

14. If a pet deposit has been paid, then we allow a **maximum** of *one medium to large dog and one cat per property **or** two small-medium size dogs **or** two cats.* For any pets or combination of pets, please **request BEFORE moving in or before purchasing pets**. Failure to do so will be a breach of contract and you agree to one month's notice to vacate the property and end the tenancy.

    You want to meet all pets that move into the property. If it's a dog, I always go around a few times, take a couple of treats and get them used to me. This is especially beneficial if they are going to grow into a bigger dog.

15. If applicable and utilities are included, water is capped at an average use; Internet and cable are at basic levels so any overage is to be paid for by the tenant; and by signing this you agree to do so. Electric is capped at _____ per month. Any month in which this is over, the tenants agree to pay the difference. The overage is split _____ between (where applicable) units, unless there is an excessive difference between one unit and the other. This is monitored. The decision of the property manager is final and you agree to these terms by signing this agreement. Natural gas, if included, is also capped at_____

    We have some suited units where separating the utilities was either not possible or not feasible at the time. To that end, when we do include utilities, we cap them. We explain that this is to prevent them from bringing family over to use their dryer, and it makes them energy conscious—so they do not have the heat on full blast and the windows wide open, or the cooling at -10 in the summer with doors open. We also want them to make sure they turn lights off and are greener for the planet (and our pockets). We can also budget what we will be spending. If they go over that, they can pay the extra as dictated above. Failure to pay results in a 10-day notice here in B.C. As utility costs increase, yours do not; this is another way of increasing "rent" without increasing rent. We "sell" this to the tenants by promoting energy efficiency and a greener planet—we haven't had anyone argue with that yet!

16. If this is a shared unit, any conflicts between the units that escalates to where verbal or physical abuse is used, then one month's notice to vacate the property for cause (eviction) will be given to the offending party(ies) as determined by the property manager, and you agree to accept this notice.

WE DO NOT TOLERATE bad language, verbal abuse, or name calling of any nature between tenants in other units, or towards the property manager or owners of the buildings. *We did not have this addendum until one day when we were evicting a tenant in a fourplex because the arguments between units were getting out of hand. As we served the notice, we explained it was because of the conflict that she had to leave. She started to get upset, naturally, and said it was the other party who caused it, then she screamed at the top of her "deep for a lady" voice, F****ing C*!*s! Yes, the C -word. I explained calmly that it was that kind of behavior that got her the notice, and regardless of what they said or did, her reactions were getting her evicted. Needless to say, after she left, things calmed down dramatically.*

17. We do not allow parties in our units, and an excessive amount of noise and or people will be considered as such; or if for any reason the police have to be called to a unit, you will be evicted. One month's notice for cause will be issued and you accept this term by signing below.
    This is a crafty line that can give you the power to evict. Whether it's a couple arguing, partying, or any other reason the police could be called, YOU CAN CALL THEM. Now you have your one month's notice for cause to evict.

18. Use of gardening equipment provided is for you to use, *and maintain*, in the condition you were given it. If it breaks during your tenancy for any reason other than fair wear and tear, as determined by the property manager, you are to repair or replace it with that of equal or greater value, as determined by the property manager. Failure to do so will result in eviction with a one-month's notice for cause, and you accept this term by signing below. Anything other than

normal wear and tear, i.e., if equipment is left out in the rain, cold etc., and occurs damage because of this, you will be liable for the cost to replace the item.

We grew tired of tenants not looking after brand-new lawnmowers and gardening equipment, and getting calls to repair lawnmowers due to them needing new spark plugs or fresh gas. We decided to add this to ensure they understood that they were responsible for what we provided and needed to look after it.

There are other addendums you may need to add or remove to suit your units; however, I hope these will give you a start on how to write your own and also help you to realize why you need certain things in place. Good addendums help you to be a good manager and to communicate the behavior you want from your clients. If people question why things are there, I question why they would ask that. Most normal people are happy to sign them since they have no intention of breaking any of the rules. You can say the addendums are from the "other owner," and that he or she wanted them in there. It helps you be on their side, and they will talk to you more about what they like/dislike. As this chapter is titled, communication and management are key to healthy relationships—personal, work, and in the case of your rentals, business too. Do not rush over this paperwork when moving a tenant in—take the time to answer their questions, make sure they fully understand each of the addendums and explain them fully, then have them sign each page to show they have read them.

CHAPTER 7

FINANCIAL DISASTER AVOIDANCE

Management of Your Business Finances

Whether you have one property or 1,000 properties, you are in a business—you own a business. Do you know any business that does not have management systems in place? Do you know any business that does not have good communication between the management and its clients or employees? If you do, I bet that business will not be around in a few years, and if your business operates the same way, it is unlikely it will be around in the long-term either. And do you know any business that doesn't have professional advisors? If you do, it may not be a successful business.

I am not an accountant, so this is not financial advice, and you should always seek professional advice from a certified financial professional to see if the following information is correct for *your* financial situation. That being said, here are a few things that I do, and that I recommend personally to friends of mine who invest in real estate. First of all, investing in real estate is a business—even if you have one property or a basement suite in your own home, it's a business, and you will want to treat it as such. Your tenants are your clients, and as such you have a business financial responsibility. Make sure your rental unit has its own bank account that is only used for that business, and if you have to use your personal credit card, pay yourself back the exact amount from the house/ business account so all the numbers match in case you're audited. Each property should have its own account!!

Second major step: get an accountant, but not just *any* accountant. My advice would be to get an accountant who also has real estate property as an investment, because even though all accountants follow the same rules, how they apply those rules depends on their personal preferences. If you have an accountant unfamiliar with the ins and outs of owning property, they will always exercise caution to make sure they don't lose *their* licence. This could cost YOU money; potentially thousands of dollars. But an accountant who also invests in real estate will understand the complexities and emotions of dealing with tenants/clients. And most importantly THINK like a real estate investor

Hire the right one for you—understanding who your clients are and the people you need on your team is also crucial to preventing you from potentially leaving money on the table, so to speak. You accountant, just like your joint venture partners if you have them, should also understand your mentality regarding the viewpoint of tenants as clients, and you operating truly as a business. Here is a story about how much it can cost you if your accountant thinks differently. Understand that neither way is incorrect; it is just different.

I have a joint venture partner with a different accountant than mine. My accountant owns 17 rental properties and he understands that the "tenants" are his clients. So, he runs it like a business, and he understands the game. On the other hand, my JV partner's accountant owns zero properties. She was recommended to him through a friend, and she used to work for the CRA (Canada Revenue Agency). Based on that information alone, he hired her; and my question to him was: So all people who work for the government are great and at the top of their game? And all people who work for the CRA for years have the mentality of the taxpayer as their priority or that of the government? And all government employees are the *best* in their field? (You can chuckle if you like.) Now I am not saying she is not good; I am merely pointing out that she may think differently based on her life experience.

This JV and I did a few properties together. I submitted all the receipts, spreadsheets, income and expenses, and bank statements, all reconciled to receipts and spreadsheets. The following year I was looking at his returns, and his expenses were way lower than I had given him. I questioned this, and he did not know why. We made an appointment with his accountant, and at the meeting I had all the paperwork from my side. Then when we got to expenses, I asked why she had not submitted them for my JV partner? She said it was to be cautious in case we got audited. (What field had they worked in previously?)

I then explained that if we *did* get audited, it would be okay, since we had done everything by the book and had all the receipts and account data clearly organized. She agreed, then submitted the following year for my partner. Had I not questioned his returns, he would have missed out on about $4,000 dollars owed to him. Do that every year for 20 years during the time you own your properties? *That's $80,000 the government would have had that my JV partner was legally entitled to.* So why did his accountant do this? Because she thought like the government, not like an investor.

So, consider finding someone who invests *and* is a great accountant, and use them—and these days we can scan and send receipts anywhere in the world, so they do not have to be in your town.

On another note, I would also find an accountant who takes the time to find out what you want to achieve and offers advice and solutions for getting there. I have had a couple of accountants who are good at accounting, yet they didn't offer me any advice, so to me that is just bookkeeping.

Expenses

Very often we do not even realize the expenses that we incur when we have a business, i.e., ink for the home printer, internet and office space, driving around to rentals for inspections, and the wear and tear on our cars, oil changes, maintenance...all of these are deductible to a certain extent. I have an app on my phone called Mile IQ (see references for details), which automatically tracks *all* my drives, and then I classify them later in the week. Also, some regular journeys it can auto-classify for you. It also gives you monthly reports and annual reports, great for your accountant to help claim back mileage, and therefore money in your pocket. This is all done through my smart phone.

There are various rules regarding many expenses, and if you are unclear, your accountant should be able to explain them to you.

We keep track of our expenses using spreadsheets and apps, along with reconciling our bank accounts to all of our receipts. If we go out for lunch or dinner with anyone that we talk about business with, guess where those receipts go? Ever go anywhere to look at real estate with a view to buying a place and renting it out? Say in Mexico? Even if it didn't work out, the fact that you went to see if it was feasible means that you can write it off—accommodations, food (not your kids' portion), but if you *legitimately* had the intent of looking to buy, it *could* be tax deductible. I'm not saying write your annual holiday off; but I am saying that if you can tie where you want to go on holiday with work, now you have some legitimate tax-deductible expenses.

Remember—everyone's personal tax situation is different, so just because it applies to someone and works for them does not mean it applies to and works for you. There are some things, however, that because you own rentals, are standard expenses and deductions across the board. The interest on your mortgage is usually tax deductible against the income the property generates, with the variable being how you borrowed the money and where from. Even though you may cash flow every month $400-$500 in your pocket, your profit may be close to zero by the time your accountant does their magic and allows for things that are permitted under the regulations.

The thing to be very cognizant of is that there are rules *you have to follow* in order to ensure you comply with the law. *Never* break the law. If people say you can do this or that, verify it with your accountant before jumping in. The laws do allow for growth, and they want people like you to provide housing stock. They are trying to close loopholes which unscrupulous people use to prevent paying taxes, so again this is another reason it is so important to have a savvy accountant. Taxes mean we live in a society that has things we can use: schools, hospitals, parks, police, roads, and basically everything we utilize every day. Paying taxes is not bad; in fact, it is good—it means you are earning money, and the higher the bracket, the more money you earn so you should want to be in the higher tax bracket! But overpaying taxes is bad! That is when you pay and you do not have to, effectively giving the government extra money to spend very wisely as they always do, right? As a business owner, it is your responsibility to ensure that you are paying the *right* amount of taxes, and a great accountant will help you do that efficiently.

Property management

When I say "property management," I mean actual *financial management* of the physical property and not the tenant. Nearly all of our properties have things in them that will have a limited life expectancy—some will be longer and some will be shorter. When we, as landlords, get stressed and create problems for ourselves, is when something happens that we were not expecting, and now we have to pay for it and money is tight. Or, something breaks and we don't have time to go fix it. Now imagine this scenario instead: The phone rings. You glance down and see it's one of your tenants. You answer and they tell you that the water tank has burst; or the heating system, which was aging, has finally died and it's the coldest day of the year.

The usual response is a churning stomach and the thought, "How the heck am I going to get that fixed?" Now imagine if you had a system where either the maintenance picked up on the age and replaced it before the problem occurred, or you were sitting with more than enough capital in the business account to cover it, so all you had to do was make a couple of phone calls, totalling maybe half an hour max, and the issue would be resolved! And it was all resolved while you were carrying on with whatever it was that you find important in your life. Which of the two would you prefer? The second one every time, right?

A good accountant who understands rentals and can help advise you and set up a planned maintenance budget, and having good management systems in place around your financials and your clients will help prevent stress when things go awry. Remember: It's not your client's fault you bought cheap taps or a second-hand washing machine that is now broken again. It all ties into the picture of managing your clients and how well you are managing them.

Good property management comes down to good planning and organization. When we set up our joint venture accounts, we ensure that as part of the renovation and closing costs, we have an amount that will cover any unforeseen emergencies such as those above. Everything that has a shelf life should be on a spreadsheet, with the current age and expected replacement date: roof=20 years, HVAC systems=10 years, hot water tank=10 years, siding (dependent on type) cleaned and refinished every three-five years or more often, depending on the area. Inspections and maintenance conducted annually—HVAC, windows, gutters, drains, electrical inspections. Painting of walls every three years, dependant on tenant turnover and flooring lifespan, and then some of the big-ticket items—washer, dryer, dishwasher, stove, microwave. Planning for all of these, on a spreadsheet, allows you to see, *and plan* when you should be replacing items; and it will help you track work to see if certain things are breaking sooner than they should, thus allowing you to investigate why, and to be preventative rather than reactive. An example of this would be taps—you might find yourself replacing faucets in a building more often than would be normal. How many people keep track of tap replacements? It could be that the city water pressure has increased due to upgrades, and now you need to install a pressure reducer to prevent plumbing fixture breakdowns. You probably would not see this unless you were tracking replacements vs. life expectancy of fixtures and fittings.

What we monitor we can improve on, and ultimately the financials of your rental property should be right up there at the top of your priorities. When it comes to headaches and stress around rentals, I have always found it is ***money*** that creates the emotion and stress; and when you are emotional and stressed, it is 99 percent of the time directed at the tenant.

"I need a tenant because I can't afford two mortgage payments." Remember that desperation creates bad decision-making in tenant selection.

"They keep breaking these, so I will put a cheap one in." (When a really good one may last a lifetime. "Again, this will cause stress, where if you purchased a higher quality item, you'd be able to feel peaceful about that issue..)

These are a couple of examples of why it is important to track monthly expenses, and to compare one year to the next to see where you can improve, *and save time and stress.*

CHAPTER 8

HELP ME! — WHEN TENANTS GO WILD

You've done it all—bought the right house, screened well for a good tenant, and even viewed them as a client. They were awesome, and everything was peachy, and then something happened!

Despite all our best efforts, there is always the possibility that at some point the tenant will go crazy, or start doing crazy stuff, and worst of all, damage the unit or not pay the rent. What then? Well there are options and there is hope....

The big bad Tenancy Branch!

Love them or loath them, the Tenancy Branch (or your local equivalent) is, and will be, an integral part of your business. The Tenancy Branch, the organization that 99 percent of places have, is charged with regulating the client/tenant relationship and ensuring both sides operate within the law. This will be the organization that you, or your tenant, can make formal complaints to about each other, and it is the first step to the resolution of any issues.

Most people I know who own rentals have never even read the Tenancy Act, which is the law and the legal rules for being a housing provider and renting to people in the area. They have a belief system that the Tenancy Branch is purely for the tenants, is against landlords, and all the other horror stories we all tell ourselves about the organization.

However, the Tenancy Branch also provides the forms for tenancy agreements and move-in inspections, the forms to use when serving tenants notices, and also for tenants serving *you* notices. Everything has a very specific procedure, and the Tenancy Branch is the organization that helps disseminate that information and also helps to resolve disputes.

I am here to tell you that the Tenancy Branch is *not* as big and bad as people think.

There are things I love about the Tenancy Branch, and things I don't agree with, and please note that the Tenancy Branch I speak about in this chapter is the one here in British Columbia. The one in your area, and its rules, may differ slightly. Regardless, we all have to operate within their rules, so it pays to know them *before* you need to use them. Imagine if you didn't know the rules of the road and just went out driving without taking a test, didn't know about traffic lights and what they meant, didn't know about stop signs and why they were there, and didn't know the rules at roundabouts.

I imagine it would not be long before you got a ticket from the police, or worse, were involved in an accident that cost you a lot of money. It may even put you off driving forever if the accident was bad enough. Do you want to get lessons from someone who has already had the experience of driving? Someone who knows the rules of the road? Of course, you do—that's how we learn.

Yet when we buy a rental, we often think, "Well, I have owned a house before, so I'll just buy one and rent it out," or, "I've seen it on TV How hard could it be?" But as with driving, you should get your advice from, and benefit from, the experience of people who have walked the walk successfully, such as other investors who are willing to listen to you and to coach you to become the "driver" you need to be to steer your rental houses to success, especially when dealing with the Tenancy Branch!

Cleaning your windows: How knowing the tenancy rules can save you time, money and stress!

The Tenancy Act is a pretty easy read; not a bunch of legal jargon you can't understand. When you read it, you will realize there are a few things that actually help you and save you money. Like the time a tenant wanted me to go clean the mildew off her aluminum windows that she had let become black with mold after we had given her a spotless house. I nearly went at my own expense and time before remembering the Act. Then I re-read it and learned that it was actually in favor of the landlord. I kindly printed it off, highlighted the section explaining the rules, looked up top tips to prevent and rectify the situation on Google, and gave it all to her, explaining that it was her responsibility. (This is also now part of our tenant handout folder and inspection checklists that we give to the tenant).

The Tenancy Branch wants you to try and resolve issues *before* filing, so if you have correspondence you have given your tenants with the correct information, and a paper trail of solutions you have offered them, and you still end up having to file, they will look more favorably at you. One thing to note about the Tenancy Branch, even though there is an Act for you to follow, is that the decision is made by the arbitrator (who is someone employed by the Tenancy Branch to oversee and enforce the Act when there is a disagreement between two parties). So, the decision is "in his opinion," meaning you have to follow the Act but there are variables he or she may take into consideration. You want *to make sure* that even if they consider the "sob story" of the tenant applicable, or more likely the straight-out lies they may tell (yes, tenants tell lies when trying to save themselves), you will have enough evidence to knock down anything they conjure up. **This is why it is important to keep files on all your tenants, from the beginning and even after they leave. We keep files for** *years.*

Another thing to be wary of, and this has actually cost us money—is that when you call to get advice from the Tenancy Branch, they do not always give you the correct advice! **WTF?!** I hear you say. Yes, the "experts" we call to get advice, so we as rental housing providers can do the right thing, may give us the wrong advice and it may cost us money. There really is no way to be 100 percent sure they are giving you the correct advice unless you read and know the Tenancy Act yourself, which if you are in business (which you are), it is vitally important to know the rules of the business you are playing in.

Our tenants come to the rescue!

In one situation, we had a tenant apply to move in; they got approved, we received the check for the first month's rent and the security deposit, and then a few days before he was going to move, he asked for his money back, saying he didn't want to move there.

According to the Tenancy Act, we would not be required to return his deposit, and he would still owe us the first month's rent.

This is really only fair, given that we would have rented to someone else and had this month of rent from someone else.

Even if he gave us written notice, it would need to be written notice served in accordance with the Act, which required it to be given *before* the first of the month (the effective date for the rental to commence).

Just because that was the law, it didn't mean he was happy about it; and he took the opportunity to go online and slander me, our company, and our units.

That was unfortunate, but our mindset and policy of treating our tenants like clients really shone through in this situation, because our current and previous tenants came to our online rescue and staged a retaliation against him, eventually forcing him to remove his comments. Yes!

Unfortunately, this situation escalated further and we ended up seeking a judgement against the person. Because we'd kept great records, including screenshots of his online slandering, we were able to seek some sort of justice. However, landlords are not looked upon favorably in most court proceedings, so it's up to you to make sure you have all the right paperwork completed and evidence of every single transaction and communication.

*It is important to keep files from the start on **all** your tenants, from the beginning and even after they leave. We keep the files for years.*

The Tenancy Branch and its advocates can take time to resolve issues, and it can be a slow process when things are not going the way you wish. Any time we file for an end to tenancy, even if we give them a 10-day notice, or a one-month or two-month notice, we file for possession (to get our house back). The reason we do this is: if you give, for example, a two-month notice and the tenant accepts the notice, gets to the end of the two months, and for whatever reason is unable to find a house and refuses to move, what do you do? If you file then, you will be waiting another two or three months for a hearing date. So then your two-month notice becomes a five-month wait! If this is a bad tenant, or someone not paying, now you have a very long time with a bad tenant and perhaps without rent.

There are some quicker methods if they are not paying, but expect up to three months potentially without rent. Even if it goes to hearing and you win, and the cost of bailiffs and other expenses are awarded, collecting on them through the court system might not even be worth your time and effort and stress. I am not saying this will happen; however, if you have a good business system and all your "what-ifs" are covered, you should have the contingency to cover this eventuality. If you don't, then you are only one mistake away from failure. This is why it is important to have a *minimum* of three months rent in your bank account at the *start* of the tenancy, and you want to be adding to that emergency fund *every* month. Our emergency funds in our properties are between $5,000 and $10,000 per property, depending on age and type. Call it a sleep-easy fund, or a stress-free cushion, but whatever you call it, make sure you have one!

The site for residential tenancies in B.C. that we go to first is: https://www2.gov.bc.ca/gov/content/housing-tenancy/residential-tenancies

You will want to know the one for your area and use it!

Use this for getting all the correct forms, and general information about situations, and then *always* check with the Act itself when disputes arise to make sure you follow the rules. Print off the Act and submit it to the tenant (the part that matches your situation) with your letter or letters as part of your evidence for the hearing. This proves you have done everything you can to resolve the situation and follow the rules.

I have also served a 10-day notice, for non-payment of rent, to a tenant, and she called the Tenancy Branch telling them incorrect information and then telling me that she had two months before she had to leave. The Tenancy Branch told her that she had two months to find a place because I can give only two months notice without cause. Obviously, the tenant didn't relay the "whole truth." I told her to re-read the forms, and then call the Tenancy Branch back to verify. Needless to say, she was now desperate to pay us the money, and also make up for not paying by paying next month a week early. Now imagine if you did not know the Act and the rules, and the tenant told you this—what would you have done?

Arbitration

Going to arbitration should always, in my opinion, be a last resort. As a landlord, it costs you a lot of time, headache, and money. There is almost always a way to resolve things if you communicate with your tenants. Although their frustration may be directed at *you*, typically the origin of the problem is not you. On a property we once had, every few months we would get a string of complaints, excuses, and late rent. It was always paid; however, there was always a story for why it was late—needed new tires, got laid off, switched jobs, etc., etc.

We could have issued notice to evict and we had every right to do so, but we also knew that as soon as we did, they would be filing with the Tenancy Branch as well as complaining about *everything*, and possibly not even paying rent! Knowing that this relationship was not one we wanted to continue, instead of evicting them, we went and spoke to them. We explained that the owners were getting frustrated (if it's your only unit and they know you own it, use your significant other or the other person who invested with you on this house; always have another person as it helps you deflect). We empathized with them, and we said that we knew they were frustrated with things.

Then we asked them what they thought could be a solution to everyone's problems, and they said they should look for another place. I said that if they wanted to do that, it would be okay, and that I would let them out of the lease without penalty. And I said that we could give them longer than the two-month notice period would have been. I also informed them that any late payments within the timeframe they were looking at would result in a 10-day notice. And I told them that if they left the house in great condition, I would not only give them their deposit back but an extra $500 after moving out. I knew the place would need some work anyway and I also knew it would not be that great when I got it back. I also knew that she wasn't good with money, and by my offering a little more, she was less likely to miss any other payments of rent and would at least do "her" best to clean it, hopefully saving me a couple of hundred in cleaning at least. I also knew that once she was out, because of the market rents (I inherited this tenant), we would be able to increase the rent by a couple of hundred dollars at least. So, by helping my client with an idea that *they* came up with—sure it would cost us more right now, but the business would make that back in less than two months!

Many people think counterproductively in these tense situations because they are emotional—but I want you to remember that it *is* a business! They have been your clients, and they will tell *50 other people* that you gave them *more* at move-out time. Now, how many other people are going to want to apply to your business and become your clients!

When the Tenancy Branch *does* need to be involved, keep meticulous records and any expenses you incur so you can claim them.

The reason I use the government-provided forms with addendums is because if we ever go to arbitration and I have used all their forms correctly, there is less margin for dispute from the tenant or from the arbitrator.

Now let us say you have filled all the forms and you now have a hearing date. What next? First of all, read all the paperwork and make a checklist of what has to be done and by what date. Second, read the Act and the agreements, making sure you have done everything correctly. Third, build your case. Make three copies of everything—this is usually a lot of paper even for a simple case. Once you have all your paperwork, number every page and highlight the points that support your case—in the Act, in the paperwork, and in the forms. Then prepare a pre-sheet that explains the key points throughout the file that you want the tenant and the arbitrator to look at.

Note: The arbitrator is unlikely to look at the file before the hearing, and even during the hearing he/she will flick to certain bits. This can be frustrating as you do all this work and he/she hardly looks at it. Be prepared that this may happen. And for this reason, the easier you make it for them to *glance* at the important points and facts, the better. Bullet points, page numbers, and highlighter pens help.

When hearing day finally arrives, make sure that you are somewhere where you will not be interrupted. If this is your home, make sure other phones are on silent, put the call on loudspeaker, and place copies of the paperwork on the table in front of you, as well as a few pens for making notes. We record our calls either through an app on our phone or else using our phone if we are on the house phone. I recommend a voice-recording app. They cost about $5 for a good one, but keep a history of any calls in an audio file that you can download at any time—it's worth the price of a coffee!

Do not argue with the arbitrator—only answer the questions they ask you directly. If the tenant starts to tell lies, do not talk over them. If you have done your job properly, there should be very little room for interpretation. Remember—they deal with lots of *angry callers* every day, so make sure *you* are not one of them. Be polite, professional, and if need be, highlight anything in the evidence that supports your case as you proceed.

Sometimes a decision is made instantly; sometimes you have to wait while they check the Act (even though you have it printed and highlighted for them) and then proceed to the next step. If it is for possession, they will usually give a date that the tenant has to be out by. I then speak to the tenant and try to arrange things with them based on the decision. For example, we won one case and the tenant had 48 hours to vacate. The decision was on a Thursday, so we said to the tenant, "Look, the decision has been made and we will let you have until Sunday evening to be clear." This made us look a bit better and hopefully calmed the tenant down a little so they didn't leave upset and smash things. It also hopefully prevents you from having to get a bailiff, as this is yet another expense.

The arbitrator may have had a bad day or had an argument with their spouse the night before, and this can color their decisions. Even though they are supposed to be unbiased, they are human, and giving them a reason to be emotional about a decision by pissing them off is *not* what you want to do. Always be professional, have an abundance of evidence, clearly marked out and simple to follow—it makes their job easier, you have to say less, and the decision will go your way, *if* you followed the Act!

Evictions after the Tenancy Branch has awarded you possession

It is always better if you can evict a tenant without having to go to arbitration. There are things you can legally do that may make them leave before getting this far. Be advised that if you are not comfortable or if the tenant is aggressive towards you, *do not place yourself* in a situation where you could be harmed. If necessary, have someone else capable of performing these actions *or* hire a professional. Know the rules, and by "know the rules" I mean ***know the rules***—this is your strongest advantage, and when people understand you know the rules, they very often do not argue (or they go to Google and get misinformation from another state or province that is different to the rules in your area!).

You can demonstrate that you know the rules by being professional from the beginning, having all the forms filled out, having tenant handout folders, and using all the official paperwork for *every* occurrence. When things start to drift and go awry, issue the correct paperwork *and* a letter explaining the paperwork that has been issued, what they can do to rectify, and the timeframes they have to follow. Also include the possible consequences if the rules are not followed, and the solutions you have recommended. The Tenancy Branch likes to see that you have tried to rectify the situation and resolve the issue.

Even if Uncle Johnny passed away, the dog ate the cat, the kids needed a new $500 remote control drone, the car blew up, a divorce is in progress, and any other excuse they conjure up, follow the rules and issue all the paperwork to the tenants required by the Tenancy Branch the day it is due. If you choose not to follow through and they are genuinely going through a rough patch, you can be lenient, but not with the paperwork. The *paperwork* is your silver bullet if things escalate.

Next, be firm but fair, but that doesn't mean be soft and emotional. Be firm about what you want and your expectations, and stick to them. If things are not followed through, then issue eviction paperwork. If you ask for a repair to be made because angry boyfriend kicked in a door, understand that it's traumatic, but you will still issue the notice of repair, and then you can explain why it needs to be fixed with a timeframe that is reasonable—if it's not a safety issue, perhaps six weeks. This gives people enough time to repair it. If they are unable to afford to fix the door, for example, then have them sign to say they agree that if you pay for it they will pay you back, and then agree on a timeframe or a payment schedule. Have them sign, and give a copy to both parties.

Then if they do not stick to the schedule, issue an eviction notice. Being proactive is also something you must do when they request reasonable repairs. You can't take two years to fix a dripping tap and expect them to fix something in two days. Be consistent.

Have a professional deal with the eviction if you feel uncomfortable doing it yourself. This shows the tenant you mean business, and because they are a third party, it makes it easier for you to "side" with the tenant. You can tell them you're "…just doing your job but these are the rules." There is less chance of error on the paperwork using a professional, and to the tenant you look like you have hired (because you have) a professional to deal with them.

If they are being difficult and you just want them out, you can start doing monthly inspections *every* month, and taking the full hour to do so. Go at dinner time or in the morning. According to the rules, there are set times when you can go in, but the idea is to be as much of a nuisance, within the guidelines, as possible.

There are positive methods that can also work and should always be tried first, when giving notice. Offer to cover the cost of a removal van, or a moving-out fee given to them before or on time in accordance with the notice, even if you give them notice for cause. Give them a letter when you give them notice for cause, and on the letter state, "If you leave in accordance with the notice and there is no damage, we will not only refund your deposit but give you an extra $400." You could even say: "If you move out on time, I'll give you $300; if you're a week early, $500!" Even if they leave and you have to clean and do some minor repairs, this is far less costly and less stressful than having a bad tenant stick around.

CHAPTER 9

THE KEY TO SUCCESS: EDUCATION AND GROWTH

"When you know better, you do better."
– Maya Angelou

I thought this topic deserved a whole chapter to itself because of the impact it can have on your real estate business, and on your relationships around that business, both at home *and* with the tenants.

Many people think education stops when they leave the "educational system," but the truth is that's just where it begins. Ask yourself what made you want to have a rental property? Was it the potential money you could earn? Was it security for the future? Was it a safer place to put your hard-earned money instead of the volatile stock markets? Was it to balance out your portfolio? Whatever the reason, you were probably *taught* that belief, or educated somewhere by someone about the benefits, or else you would not have taken the leap and started.

Everyone is educated to some extent about the benefits of real estate. Those who are educated about the negative benefits never invest; those who are educated about the positive benefits ei-

ther invest or want to, yet it's those who understand **both sides and manage both correctly who succeed in this field.**

Ask yourself who educated you about real estate. Where did you get your education from? What was the belief system you were "taught," and have you stuck with that belief system forever? Who educated you about dealing with tenants? Dealing with people? Dealing with yourself? Many of these lessons are inherited from our family and friends and closest associates. Very few people actually go out, spend more money on their education for the above topics, and improve by learning from successful people who are better at it or more experienced than they are. The more educated you become, and the better perspectives you get about rental property and dealing with tenant clients, the more successful you will become in your business. The better your business and the more success you have, will equal less stress and more money in your pocket.

Imagine paying $10,000-$30,000 per year to be educated by your friends or family, as opposed to going to college or being taught by experienced professionals. You wouldn't! You'd want to be educated by experts in the field. Now let's go a step further—after paying all this money to get book smart, what do you do next? You try to find a job in the field and then gain the *experience* to become competent at it. Or even worse, you take a job in another field not even related to your education and work your way up from the bottom. Getting the right education at the right time can save you thousands and make you millions, as any long-term real estate investor can attest to. If you get the wrong education in real estate, it can cost you many thousands of dollars and missed opportunities. Getting the right education, on the other hand, not only creates millions of dollars of wealth but the priceless value of a stress-free life and *time* to live your life. Real estate, when done correctly should help you *live* your life, not *be* your life!

With real estate and personal development there are so many courses, programs, and false promises of getting rich quick. So, it is understandable why people shy away from education in real estate. I spend, on average, between $10,000 and $30,000 *every year* on furthering my education, which includes memberships in a couple of local groups where, when I need it, I can get advice from people who are experienced and successful at what I am trying to accomplish. Once you figure out what you want real estate to accomplish for you, make sure you connect with like-minded individuals in organizations that match your goals and budget. It is no use to me (being from the UK) to hire an elite-level ice hockey coach and paying that price, when all I need is the local skating coach to get me to the next level. It doesn't mean that the NHL coach couldn't or wouldn't be able to get me there; it means that I do not need to spend that much money at this point!

As a side note, the value of the price of training is what you get back in return—the return on your investment. Once I spent $10,000 on a program. I flew down to the United States to take it—so flights plus hotels—and at the end of the course, the systems they "promised" would work didn't quite pan out. I felt that I had wasted my money. Yet a few years later, one little thing that I learned there enabled me to negotiate on a joint venture, which became four rentals. Today they are worth $200,000 in equity and growing.

It is better to have the knowledge and not need it, rather than need it and not have it. People say knowledge is power, but knowledge is not power—*applied knowledge is power.* But if you don't have it to apply at the right *time*, what is the long-term cost and loss?

Where should I find education?

What kind of education would I recommend? Well, you should mix up what you are doing—there is free education, researching things yourself like reading the Tenancy Act, joining on-line groups and meet-up groups, and having discussions with like-minded individuals. Then there are memberships and groups you can be part of that come with benefits. I am a member of REIN Canada (Real Estate Intelligence Network) which, I believe, is Canada's largest and one of the longest running groups of real estate investors. I strongly recommend that you look into this as a huge resource, and any quality group like this will be an invaluable part of your team. Here are the top benefits you would receive from joining a group like REIN, and why I personally recommend them.

- Discounted Insurance with superior coverage
- Networking with like-minded people who can help you on your journey
- Education about your business and how to be more successful
- Research analysis helping you to make superior purchase choices and management decisions
- Support on your journey
- Celebration and recognition of your successes.

The cost of savings by being a member pays for the membership threefold. The benefits include acquiring a lot of knowledge, networking with like-minded people, and saving money! A triple win for you. Of course, there are other groups and organizations that may better for you, or more local to you, but this one definitely works for me and they are by FAR the leaders in research.

REIN's website is: www.reincanada.com.

As with anything, you need to be part of a group or meetup that resonates with you and your goals *and* that can provide you with measurable *financial* benefits, not just ones that make you feel good! Visit a few different groups and try before you buy.

Landlord BC is another organization I would consider. Although they somewhat side with the tenant, they do know the rules and they offer education. Again, this depends on your budget and business expenses. Remember—if you have profit and cash flow from your rental, use that money to pay for it—let the tenant pay for your education!

Then there are specific programs that offer more specialized knowledge about certain things, like rent-to-owns, how to buy your first property, fix and flip, and many more. If these are the strategies you are using in your rental portfolios, then look for them. Revnyou, our company, has a program called from "Rookie to Rock Solid Real Estate Investor," designed to help you get your first property, or to transition from a dabbler to a professional. We also have a program called R.E.A.P. (Real Estate Achievement Program), which is a one-year subscription program where we coach and teach people for a whole year how to be successful real estate investors. It costs only $197 a month with a money back guarantee.

Most courses cost in the range of a few thousand to ten thousand dollars each. Some promise magical returns in two weeks or two months, and with all the reality TV shows out there now, people are a somewhat misled about what it takes to succeed in real estate. Remember that *it's a business* however you do it, and like any business there are start-up costs, running costs, growing pains, and all other things associated with a new business. That does not mean you shouldn't sign up; it just means be cautious and get feedback from someone who has done the program that you're considering—how did it work for them (which doesn't mean it will work for you, but you can listen to what they have to say)? Do they offer any guarantees? If you do an online search, is there negative press about it? Again, this does not mean it's bad. I just came back from an "Unleash the Power Within" with Tony Robbins, and some parts of it got some bad press, but for me the event was life-changing. So, take everything you see and read, and make an educated decision—not an emotional one about getting rich quick or changing your life in a month!

In real estate, there are *two* types of education that I would recommend: one is **professional education** about your trade, your business, and anything directly related to the running and managing of your real estate business and rentals. This is the "how-to" of running your rentals, and the bread and butter of learning the "business" side. The second type of education is **personal development**—this is about you, your belief systems, how you behave, how you communicate, how you negotiate, how you solve problems, and everything to do with you personally. To be truly successful, and master your craft, you will need to pursue *both* types of education.

We have never come across anyone who is successful in real estate, or any business for that matter, that does not invest in *both*. If you want to be successful in your business (which I hope you do; otherwise, why have one?) you will need to seriously consider stepping up in these areas. Again, you don't need an NHL coach to start, unless you're at that level or you want to get to that level quicker and can afford it! Most of us, just like you, can work our way up through the leagues.

$64,000 saving?

Education can also help you maximize the returns on your property. Imagine that you have your property and then you learn a technique that helps you reduce your turnover, saving you $2,000 per year; and you also receive a business tip that saves you $1,000 per year. Over 20 years, that's $64,000 dollars extra in your pocket! Now how much was it worth paying for that education/knowledge?

I personally had this experience when someone showed me how to joint venture, partnering with others either as the money partner, or as the real estate expert in real estate. I now very rarely invest my own money, yet I still control and own a large portfolio by giving my expertise to others who have the capital to invest. The return on that education for me has been worth millions of dollars—and it only cost me ten thousand dollars!

This is the power that education—the right education—can have; it translates to money in your pocket. Every year I learn something new that propels me to another level, either personally or professionally—which is why I invest so much time in education for myself and for my business, and a huge reason why I suggest that you do too. However, there are some things to be wary of when looking at training—like promises of *getting rich quick, $$$$$ in weeks with no effort, no actual real estate knowledge required*, etc., etc. Any business takes knowledge and effort, and work skills and people skills to be successful. Real estate investing and managing property and tenant/clients is no different.

FACT: Once your business is up and running, it may be easier to get to a hands-off position when it comes to managing the business, but do not kid yourself! Unless you are prepared to do the work *after* you finish your day job and put the necessary time in to prevent you from losing money, time and/or your sanity, then do not get sold on the *hype* that some courses offer!

Even if you want to be *involved* in real estate, yet do not have the time, personality, or patience required, and therefore you have decided that *a joint venture* is the way to go, I would still recommend a level of education that allows you to have an educated discussion with your partner that you are joint venturing with. When we joint venture with people, we have a program you can take online or during our retreat weekends. It's called "Rookie to Rock Solid Real Estate Investor." We make sure that *everyone* who works with us takes this program. We do not charge our joint venture partners, obviously, but it ensures that when we talk about a property, everyone understands what we are saying, and it does not sound like gobbledygook! It also helps joint venture partners that we work with understand the way we think. Imagine if you had the wrong types of joint venture partners, and all they cared about was the money, and they did not care about the clients you had to deal with. Their decisions would be based only on their perspective, wants and needs.

It should be of *great* importance to you that anyone you work with also thinks of tenants as *clients* and also understands that you are running a business and that the clients are the *lifeblood* of that business. If you are going to buy rentals and manage the business with other people, your potential partners have to know not only about real estate, but also how to deal with and manage clients in a respectful and appropriate way. This is critical!

Imagine taking your car to a garage and not knowing a single thing about cars or engines—how easy would it be for the mechanic to overcharge you? Or to tell you something you simply do not understand? With a car, this can cost you a few hundred dollars, or maybe even a few thousand; and in a property, this can cost you hundreds of thousands to millions of dollars! Educate yourself *and your partners* about the business! It will greatly increase your chance of success.

Also, to prevent miscommunication, you want all of your people to be educated so you speak the same language. Some of our real estate coaching clients are happy to work with us with an open checkbook because we have developed a level of trust over the years, but for most people, we like them to have at least a certain level of understanding. We first educate our joint venture partners, tell them what is in it for us, what is in it for them, the upside, the possible downside, and the expected outcomes based on our extensive experience. We also educate them on worst-case scenarios, the "what-if" situations, and then we explain the course of actions if the "what-if" happens. Imagine trying to work with a partner who had no clue about what you were saying, or worse, you have no clue about what *they* are saying. That is another huge reason to be educated. And it is also a benefit to be part of organizations like REIN as they have people who can help you through *any* situation, and they very often have paperwork to help educate you and your clients.

Do you need to master anything before taking action *towards* investing and managing? The short answer is, "No." Action trumps inaction every time! Action will help you gain knowledge—even if you make a mistake. Action will give you an education, and some of this may be in the form of expensive mistakes, but you will learn from them! You will want to *minimize* the cost of those mistakes and improve each time you do something, which is where groups and memberships can definitely help guide you, and where courses can offer you knowledge to get you up and running. But it is always *experience* that will offer you the means to be truly successful.

I hope this section highlights the value of education and of experience, and the importance of the bottom line, which is money in your pocket to give you the choices you deserve in your life.

CHAPTER 10

CREATING VALUE AND FINDING OPPORTUNITIES

A lot of people ask, "How do you find deals?" Well, the truth of the matter is, sometimes they come along, but most of the time, they're *created*—created through adding value and opportunity for the house, for your investor (even if that's you), and your tenant.

"What? Create value for your tenant?" I hear you ask. Yes. Create value for your tenant. Remember—they are your *client*, and without a *client/tenant*, I do not care how good your house is or what area it's in; without them giving you money *every* month, your business dies.

Now the question to ask yourself is: What does your client value? If your client values a nice family home and they have kids, they would most likely value a fenced-in yard. How much does it cost to build a fence? $2,000-ish. Is it worth spending that amount of money to ensure you have a good family for your investment? If they leave, you could lose that cost just in the turnover; saving one turnover could pay for the fence.

Oftentimes, people look at the hard cost instead of the potential savings by *creating value*. Very often I see people not allowing pets, since pets destroy places. And yes, they can, but so can *kids*. So can *adults!* In order to create value in our rentals, we allow pets. And we therefore ensure that the flooring is a better grade—and sometimes commercial grade. This way the floors last longer, can survive being peed on, or getting wet, or having things dropped on them, and they can survive heavy use. Instead of buying the cheapest things possible, we assess where wear and tear would most likely happen in a "what-if" scenario and we upgrade to something sturdier. All of this creates value to the tenant *and* the investor.

Now, how do you continue to create value for your tenant without spending a lot of time and money? For example, you can create value by differentiating yourselves from other landlords by offering value-added services at their request. How many people have the clause, "Must mow lawns"?

How does this create value-added services for the tenant? Because of this clause, a tenant might feel pressured, so you can offer them a way to pay an extra amount on their rent every month, usually $40, and then all summer you can ensure that the lawns are maintained and kept to a good standard. A few take us up on this service, and the cost to you is less than what you take over the 12-month period; we only cut lawns for about six or seven months maximum. In the summer, it's so hot it doesn't grow very much! And this creates value for the tenant because they no longer worry about the lawn, and the cost is spread out and added to the rent so they don't even notice it. As a bonus, you add value to the property because it always looks great, and you add value to the investor because they make a little extra cash flow over the 12-month term.

This is an example of value added to the tenant that does not cost you any time or money, and in fact, creates a win-win for everybody involved. And you can outsource the lawns to another company, so it provides benefits for others too.

How else can you create added value for your tenant? What value added services would they like or appreciate?

Things to make sure of when adding value:
- **It adds value in time or experience to the tenant.**
- **It adds value to the investment.**
- **It does not cost you any money from your cash flow; in fact, it should enhance it.**
- **It benefits everyone involved.**

If you focus on adding value and looking at the bigger picture—like putting in better floors and sturdier units, which may look like more cost, but in the long term ensures better tenants, less wear and tear, less repairs and more longevity—you will do okay. If all you focus on is what is in it for *you*, you might miss out on some great opportunities to improve your business.

The value add could be simply hiring a professional property manager to manage your units for you, which helps save you stress and time, ensures professional communication for the tenant, and removes you from any confrontational engagements. This can also prevent turnover and ensure vacancies are filled faster, thus reducing costs to you. Value adds have to be something that you and everyone involved sees as **value**.

Opportunity

Opportunity is defined in the dictionary as, "A set of circumstances that makes it possible to do something." Opportunity therefore, can be created, since you have the power to change your circumstances and therefore "do" something. When we talk about opportunity, we tend to consider the property and the deal, but what would you do if you thought about creating opportunity for the tenant who is your client?

Well, first they have the opportunity to rent a *quality* rental property that is a little nicer than any other in its bracket. If the home is a B home, you want to be one of, if not *the best*, home in that bracket. This gives the tenant an opportunity to have a home nicer than their friends or neighbours! It creates demand for your home if their friends see how much nicer yours is in their price bracket.

We also give tenants the opportunity to pay rent on *flexible* terms by offering bi-weekly payments to match their pay schedule. There is also an 11-month payment program where they get to have a month off from paying rent. For this program, we add the annual rent amount up and then divide by 11 months, and they have to have paid up a full year before they can use the month off. This allows them to pay a bit extra each month and perhaps have a summer month or Christmas as a break. They can also keep going and build up a credit for "in-case," because life happens. There is also a combination of the two—an opportunity that adds value by giving the tenant options and adds value to the investor since they get paid ahead of time, always.

Win-win.

We create opportunity for our current tenants by putting them on a list, and every time a home or property becomes available, they get notified *before* we market to the public. This gives them the opportunity to let a friend know about a great property—if you have good tenants they usually hang around with like-minded people. This has the advantage of adding value to the tenants by helping a friend or themselves; it adds value to the investor with lower vacancy rates due to demand for your properties; and it adds value to you due to saved time and stress marketing a property.

Creating value *inside* your home is equally as important. If you create value in the investment, the investor is more willing to spend on *other* things that improve the property and/or quality of it. Creating value in your property is also a good way to increase the revenue and income from a house. Our strategy is: We buy single family homes built around 1970, renovate with new electrical, plumbing, roof, windows, yard—basically as much as we can—and then we put a suite in the basement. This generates extra income from a space that would otherwise be underutilized. It also provides more affordable accommodations for a single professional or couple who want to have something more than a condo yet aren't quite able to step up to a full house.

This strategy alone creates an extra $850-$1,500 per month from a property and usually costs us an extra $20,000-$30,000 at the time of renovation. How would your investment in a single-family home perform with an extra $1,000 a month going into it? Over 20 years, if rents never increased, that's nearly *a quarter of a million dollars extra* into your pocket!

Now, is it worth looking at ways to create extra value?

Let's talk about that detached garage: instead of just handing the keys over to whoever rents, consider renting it out as a workshop or separate storage agreement for someone. This alone can make you $100-$300 per month. Over twenty years at top dollar, that's over $70,000 dollars. Creating value in the home, just with the extras like having a garage as storage, as mentioned above, comes to over $300,000 dollars of extra income. Now imagine re-investing the extra income—how much would it be worth over 20 years? Half a million? Would you like an extra half a million in twenty years?

Now ask yourself again: what can YOU do to create extra value, and to create *more opportunity* in your rental? **Value** and **opportunity**—two very powerful words when you focus on them for your clients.

More grass...

Now when we add value and it is an expense to the tenants, like paying for lawns getting cut, we do not focus on the cost but on the *benefit*. Someone once said to me: "When we go on holiday, we do not focus on the type of plane and the cost, we focus on the *destination*—the beach, the warm sun, the relaxing, the benefit! This is what makes the cost seem worth it, and how we get there is not something we emphasize."

Well, in this case, the plane is the *company* we use and how it gets done. I will tell you that nobody cares. The cost? Tenants might say they love doing the lawn themselves and for a few this might be true, but most people if they won some money tomorrow in the lottery would probably not be cutting their own grass.

What *we* do is focus on the free time they will have to do whatever they want, the nice lawns someone else is creating, and a cost that will become part of a payment they will not even notice. But they will enjoy the free time in the summer when they do not have to worry about the lawns being cut every week/month, or letters from the landlord about the grass, and last but not least, the possibility of something happening where they are unable to cut the grass due to holidays, bad back, illness, or something else, and then it gets done and becomes an extra expense that they didn't plan for that month.

So, when we arrange for the lawns to be cut, for our tenants it means: peace of mind, quality of lawn, headache-free, no fiddling with mowers or filling with gas, or getting out the equipment and putting it away, or maintaining the gardening equipment—all these headaches are removed for one simple low payment spread over the year! Create the reasons they *want* the value and they will happily pay for it!

CHAPTER 11

A FIRE, TWO FLOODS, A DRUG HOUSE, AND A DEAD GUY

The title of this book is about helping you to reduce stress and save money, yet even as a seasoned player in the game, there are times when we wonder what is going on—and this chapter is about a month that I hope *never* repeats itself! But it could! Applying everything in this book can help you deal with all the issues that I have encountered over the years; maybe not *prevent* them all, but certainly reduce stress by a significant amount. If nothing else, if you are having a bad week or month with your rentals, re-read this chapter and take some comfort in the knowledge that there is *always* someone worse off!

The police officer was standing at the door of a rental unit under our management, heaving and unable to enter the property due to the putrid stench emanating from inside. I leaned over and offered him a candy.

"You're eating a candy!" he cried out. I told him I had a choice: that I could either have the taste of pear drops (my favorite UK candy) in my mouth, or the smell of the guy. He took a candy!

I'd suspected something was not quite right after a couple of days at one of the units in a multi-family building we managed, so I picked up the keys from our key box and went around to let myself in. As the door opened, the heat that hit me in the face was like stepping off a plane into a hot country when you go on holiday and the humidity wafts over you. What's more, the smell was so bad that I was knocked back a few steps, and I knew instantly that something was very, very wrong. What I was *not* expecting was the smell from a body that had been decaying for over three weeks! The room was dark with the curtains closed and my eyes could not recognize anything. My other senses were so overwhelmed that I couldn't stay long enough to let my eyes adjust.

I went to get a flashlight so I could see, and I stood at the door and panned the room, looking left to right, then up and down, several times. My brain was not registering what my eyes were seeing, but then it did. I saw the white cheeks, and that's when my brain was finally able to process the image. It was in fact the *only* part of his body that was still white as it was the highest point. He was lying face down in a praying position, and the rest of his body looked like a pile of blankets – a very dark blue and black pile of blankets.

I called the police and they arrived quickly, taking statements, processing the scene, and doing whatever police do when they deal with these situations.

This was week four, and the worst week of my property management, and the biggest month of "learning."

Week one started with a phone call from my cousin and business partner Craig, who also invests in real estate in our town. He was leaving to fly to Mexico in about 20 minutes. "My house is on fire!" he shouted into the phone, in a "why the f**k is this happening now'" kind of voice. I went to the house, met him there as the firemen were coming outside so they could breathe, and smoke was still billowing from the unit. I asked him to sign a piece of paper saying I could deal with his insurance and told him to go get on the plane…which he did!

Having the right people on your team and the right insurances is huge!

I dealt with the tenants and the insurance while he was away, and it became clear what had caused the fire. One of the tenants had put something on the stove and then went into the bedroom and rolled a fatty (a joint). We later found the half-rolled fatty still on the tray at the walk through—see the pictures below:

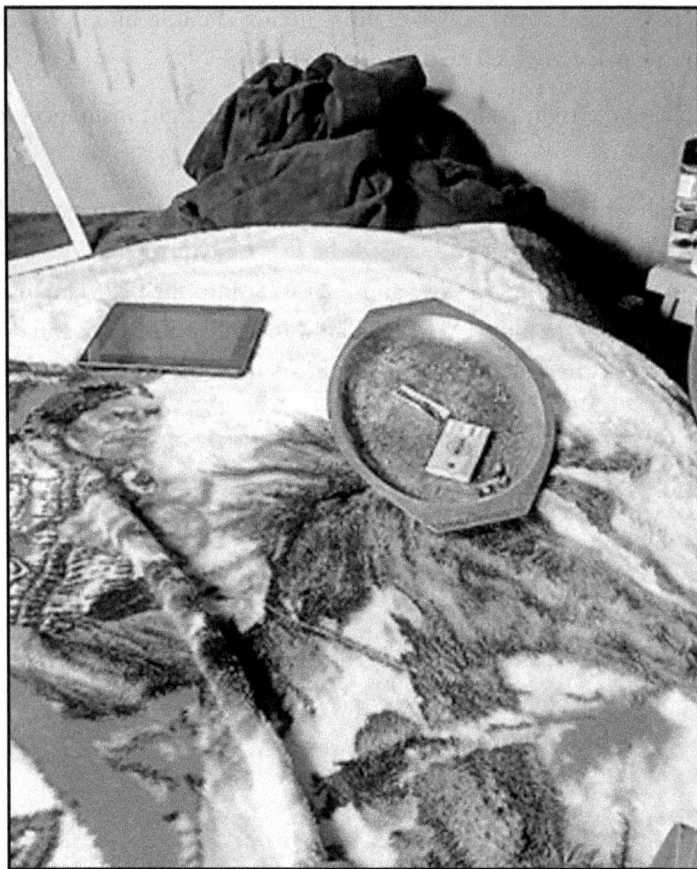

Then he forgot about the stove and it set itself on fire! As the house went up in flames, he ran out, leaving all the evidence on the bed. We also spoke to the tenant and he gave us a confession, not realising that we were filming the conversation at the time. One of the tenants announced that the other one had gone into the bedroom to get stoned and left the pan on the stove. I asked him to clarify this, and I said, "So basically, your roommate went into the room after putting a pan on the stove, was busy getting stoned, and he set the house on fire…."

The roommate looked sheepish, and then he looked up at his friend as he said in a clear voice, "Yep, and that's not the first time either, but the last time we managed to put the pan out." I appreciate when tenants are clear about what they did—it helps the insurance!

When we were back at the house after the fire was completely out, the tenant remarked that he thought Craig (the owner and my cousin) should be there more, and care about his property more. The tenant was annoyed that he was not there and that he had to deal with me instead.

I very firmly told the tenant that when Craig had booked his holiday, he had not planned on a stoner tenant burning down his investment on the day he was leaving; otherwise he would have booked it for the day after! With some tenants, their belief is that the world revolves around them; they have a high level of expectancy. So, it is important for you, the owner, to be clear and firm when dealing with what are highly stressful situations.

We met the loss adjuster the next day, and due to the age of the building we suspected asbestos in the structure (which proved to be true), so I refused the tenants entry to go back in and get their stuff unless they had all the correct protective gear and masks. As the responsible person for the property, and a business owner, you, the landlord, have a liability for the health and safety of your tenants, and you could be liable if you make a mistake!

Again, the tenants were annoyed that I didn't want to let them potentially die! They did not have tenant's insurance either, which meant that they were responsible for clearing out all their belongings before our insurance could commence remedial actions. I am always shocked by what people value at such times. I actually felt bad for them as they had lost everything, and all of it could have been replaced if they had tenant's insurance for around $20 a month. We always insist that our tenants have insurance as part of the material term of the tenancy agreement; however, Craig had inherited these tenants with the house so he could not enforce that.

Week two was the "drug house." Well, there were actually *two* drug houses, both on the same street, three doors apart. Where can we begin on these charmers? The first one belonged to a friend I used to work with many years ago; it actually used to be the family home that he grew up in, before he rented it out. He messaged me, asking me to help him file paperwork and remove some really bad tenants (druggies) who were scamming the system, destroying his house, and not paying rent. The perfect combo, right? I agreed and I helped him dot the i's and cross the t's and submit the paperwork.

At this point, the tenant was fraudulently filling tenant applications to the government, collecting welfare checks for people he had not agreed to rent to, and not paying her full rent either! She was subletting while living in the house and pocketing the money—and then spending it on drugs. Within a few weeks, we had a possession order, court-ordered bailiffs due to arrive in a couple of days, and another potential bill of thousands of dollars to remove them, store their stuff, and never see that money.

I told the owner we could pay them to leave. "WHAT?!" he shouted. I told him we had a choice: either pay the bailiffs and the storage costs and have a bill of around $6,000 to $8,000; *or* pay them $2,000 and ask them to leave within 24 hours. He was reluctant at first, because he really wanted to watch them get kicked out onto the street; but realizing it would save him between $4,000 and $6,000, he made the right choice. As with anything, timing is everything: We didn't want to tell them too early that we would pay them, as they might trash the place (even more than it was already); and we didn't want to tell them just before the weekend, as we feared the "Hey, let's have the party at my house; I'm out tomorrow."

So, we waited till Monday evening around 8.30 pm, too late to organize a party, and I knocked on the door. No one came, despite me seeing five people sitting there through the window. I knocked again, and an angry looking dude came to the door. He wasn't letting me in, so I slowly edged into the foyer, explaining that I had the possession order and that the bailiffs were coming in a few days. He said that the tenant wasn't home, which we knew to be a lie, so I wrote down our terms. I wrote that the bailiffs were booked to come on Wednesday morning at 9 a.m. and that "you will be out of a home with no money and nowhere to go, and I will have to pay the bailiffs. I would rather that you receive some money to help you move, etc., and *if* you are out by tomorrow (Tuesday) at 5 pm, I will pay you $2,000 to help you."

I left it with the angry looking dude, along with my card and number, and told him to get (we will not use her real name so let's call her Jane) Jane to call me.

I had not even got back to my car, which was 20 feet away, when Jane came running out across the snow in her bare feet, shouting, "I'll take it, I'll take it!" I went back to the house with an internal smile, knowing that we were getting what we wanted. She looked at the notice I had for her to sign, saying that she agreed to leave by 5 pm Tuesday, and would give up all stake or claim to anything left behind (so we were not charged for storing their junk), and she looked at me and said: "I'll sign it if I can have an advance of $500 so I can get started on packing right now."

Giving a known drug addict $500 cash before they leave your property is obviously not a wise choice. I told her that there was no negotiation here; she either accepted the terms, or we waited and gave the money to the Bailiff instead. So, it was her choice: leave with $2,000, or leave with nothing a day later. She agreed and signed. The next day we showed up around 4 pm to see how things were progressing, and we could see by the furniture on the lawn that she was actually moving. I Informed her that we had the cash at the shop and that she could come and get it once she was completely out.

I wandered around the house looking at some of the low-lifes that she had helping her; and it was obvious that most, if not all, were also heavy users and addicts. We gave her another hour or so as she was definitely not finished, grabbed a coffee, and watched the mayhem unfold onto the lawn.

She was like a sergeant major barking orders at the workers: "COME ON, COME ON, WE HAVE TO BE OUT!" Her "workers" were literally throwing couches, beds, and everything else out onto the lawn, and once she was out, I instructed the owner to board up his house, had her sign again to agree that she was out and no longer at the property, and had no stake in the property. I went to my office, collected the $2,000 dollars, which was made up of $20 notes for $1,000 and a court order for a thousand dollars that she owed the owner. I pulled up and handed her the envelope, and she said thank you and I drove off.

Needless to say, she lost her shit when she realized the $2,000 she received was minus the $1,000 (which was only a tiny part of what she owed the owner, but all we could get on the court order at this time). I came back to the scene, and was surrounded by the druggie removal company and Jane. She was saying it was criminal what was in the envelope, and that she did not have enough to pay all the people who had helped her. I guess it is expensive to hire drug addict help to launch your stuff onto the front lawn.... Who knew?

I asked her what she needed to move on, and she said she was $200 short. I went round and spoke to the owner and got another $200. Then I gave it to her and she moved on, although her stuff was on the lawn for a couple of days with someone sleeping on the couch on the lawn for security—in February, in the snow, in Canada!

The second drug house, which was being dealt with at the same time as the first, belonged to the sister of a woman whose rental we looked after. So, again, not even a property that we managed (it would never get to that state if we did). This time it was four serious drug addicts who also had mental health issues. One was a severe hoarder; the other three were just so far gone in life that I doubted they would ever recover. This house was the worst house I have *ever* seen, even on a TV show. We had filed the correct paperwork to evict, filed all the evidence, gone to a hearing, and we *lost!* We had videos of people tweaking out on meth on the floor and of broken windows; statements about physical attacks on the previous manager; by-law fines for mess and garbage all over the yard; evidence of all the drug use, *but* apparently that is not enough to show that the landlord's property is at risk—but that is another story!

Luckily, however, one of their welfare checks went missing in a mail strike, so we were able to evict for non-payment of rent, and the process *began*. We filed the possession order at the court, got the writ of possession, and ordered the court appointed bailiffs. We then used a similar technique as we had previously, and offered them cash for the keys and for them to walk out.... This time, though things were a little different, we were dealing with very well-known criminals, thieves, and drug users, along with mental health issues. We had to be more cautious in our approach, and almost every day we were going to the house explaining what was happening, that the bailiffs were coming, and that they would be getting nothing. The cost to clear this house and store things with the bailiffs would have been in excess of $10,000 due to the amount of stuff that they had—most of it not theirs!

There was more drama and negotiation and a *lot* of hours wasted trying to talk to them and get the result we needed. Eventually I persuaded them to take our offer, with less than 12 hours till the deadline with the bailiffs. It was 12:30 am and they signed and took the money. You can view the video I took right after we got possession and before we started cleaning up:

https://youtu.be/kAZZsM6ft9o

https://www.youtube.com/watch?v=kAZZsM6ft9o

Once the clean-up commenced, the real horror started. The video does not begin to do justice to the state of this place; and what made it even harder for the team that we brought in was the number of hazards involved. They found over 8,000 needles, and someone commented on our video that they might be diabetic! No, we didn't think so; not from the times we saw them injecting heroin into their veins right in front of us...although I suppose they could have been diabetic heroin addicts.

The duty of care that the clean-up crew had to take was huge. Every item had to be hand-sorted to make sure we were not disposing of needles, as the law here states that if you dispose of dirty needles and then someone at the dump, for example, gets infected, you could go to jail. We found weapons, ammunition, homemade swords, blades, and just nasty dangerous things; also, small heroin burning cups and over 100 crack pipes.

We also gathered up 50 mountain bikes, which the police officer could not identify as stolen or even check, as it was against their privacy rights apparently. Yes, our society is messed up when the "allegedly" stolen items cannot even be checked because it interferes with the privacy rights of the junkies. At the time of writing, I am still paying to store this stuff until the 60 days are up, and of course they haven't paid us back what they owe, currently $18,475 and climbing—which is never going to happen—and then I can try and sell the stuff, as I own it at that point, or dispose of it, or call the police and see if we can find the rightful owners.

We took the seven cats that were living in absolute squalor to the SPCA; and we still have cleaners, renovators, painters, and contractors repairing the place and bills due from that. We are going to be at around $50,000 by the time it is rent-ready again. The woman who the owner had as a property manager for this place was so extremely negligent that she will be taking her to court and suing her for damages. That manager moved in four known drug addicts, did nothing to stop the place from going rapidly downhill, issued no paperwork to prevent and remediate as it descended into a nightmare, and then walked away when it was too much. And the manager complained to the owner, saying that the tenants were so bad she could not deal with them. The people *she* placed there were so bad that she, as the professional, could not deal with them!

That was two months before the month when we finally got them out. In the last month, however, one of the drug addicts forgot that she was not around, saw her, and gave her rent money…and she took it! Even though she had signed paperwork saying she was no longer the property manager. When we found out and called her, she said okay and she deposited it in the owner's bank...minus her 10 percent commission!

I told the owner she had made some very costly mistakes with this property. One was purchasing in an area because it was cheap, and not clueing into the fact that it was cheap *for a reason*. Plus, she had never visited the house, and a short visit, especially around dusk, would have clued her in to what the area was like.

Plus, she blindly hired a property manager without doing any checks. Due to her naiveté, and unfortunately due to her trusting nature, she assumed that this lady was a professional property manager, even though she was not licensed, and had no business license, no insurance, no liability insurance, and no systems in place to vet tenants—the list of red flags was endless. *Always* vet your houses, your property managers, the area you are buying in, and especially your tenants who are being placed. Even if you use management, ensure that they have systems in place, and ask for copies of the documents that anyone signs so you have them for your own records and can verify that they are filled in correctly.

Remember that *an investment property* is like having a bag of $300,000 $400,000 or $500,000 dollars sitting on the street and then asking someone to sit there and look after it. If it was actually a bag of cash, how much more care would you take regarding where you placed it? How much more care would you take about who looks after it? How much more care would you take to check out who lives in your bag of cash, and is responsible for keeping it clean and making sure the cash doesn't fall out or get damaged? Well, this bag of cash is your rental property, and the cash is made of bricks and mortar and/or wood. Look after your bags of cash!

Week three was actually pretty easy! A phone call from the basement suite at one of my rentals saying it was raining inside her house. This was a concern because it was not raining outside! I rushed over and walked into what looked like a torrential downpour coming through a doorway into the bathroom. Knowing where the plumbing was in the house from being there during the renovations, I ruled out a pipe burst and called the upstairs tenant to enquire if she was doing laundry. She went to check and I heard "Oh shit!" as she realized that the washing machine was leaking all over the floor, about two inches deep! At that point, she turned off the washing machine!

Understand that as distressing as this is as a property owner, imagine being the tenant and *your* home is now flooded, or even worse, raining inside! Very often we jump into things from "our" perspective and do not consider what is going on for them too. Upstairs she had kids' clothes that needed to be laundered for school, and work clothes so she could get to work the next day. Downstairs, she just wanted a dry bed to go to sleep in, without the sound of Niagara Falls in her home. We all wanted the same result—repaired, fixed, and back to normal.

We all have different viewpoints. Taking a little time away from a situation to gather your thoughts, devise a plan, and let them know what you are going to do to rectify the situation—and what they need to do to help *all of you* reach the desired result, helps alleviate a lot of the tension.

Pointing fingers and calling people names rarely helps in stressful situations and could definitely make matters worse. Verifying that they are still insured and did not cancel anything is a good place to start; and when they are still insured, which they should be, you can reassure them that they will be taken care of.

If they *did* cancel their insurance, now is *not* a good time to point out how bad that choice was. This flood, at the time of writing this, caused damage somewhere between $16,000 and $18,000. Luckily, I have fantastic insurance and the company is awesome, so it is times like this that remind me why insuring one's investment properly is *so critical!* In addition to everything else, you can deal with the situation, go home and go to sleep.

Believe me, not every month is like that! In fact, I have *never* had a month like that before. I hear a lot of horror stories, like the ones above, but if you buy right, manage correctly, and follow the tips in this book, you will have a very boring and uneventful rental, which is the perfect way to do it. About 95 percent of the time, buying and managing rentals is basically uneventful, and you want it to be that way! You can insure and plan for the other 5 percent of the time and still sleep easy, even if you eventually end up having your very own "month from hell."

USEFUL REFERENCES

In this chapter, I want to share the groups, books, websites, memberships, and as much stuff as possible that you can use to grow your knowledge further. Again, this list is not exclusive, and you can always add to it, which we encourage. There are, however, patterns regarding what books people read, what courses they take, and what groups they choose to attend. If you want a model for success in your chosen field, copy the people who are already successful at it and have been for years. You do not have to carve your own path—you can simply follow others who have been successful, and then adjust along the way and eventually end up with your own personal take on the business.

Websites

- www.revnyou.com: Real Estate Education (amazing tips and courses you can take). Downloadable checklists at super affordable prices
- http://www.reincanada.com: Great membership benefits and meetings
- https://canadianrealestatenetwork.com: Great free resources for investors

- https://thereinvestors.ca/
- https://www.landlordbc.ca: Resource site and membership
- https://www.statcan.gc.ca/eng/start: Government site for all forms you will need for tenancies
- https://www.tenantscreeningreport.com: Tenant verification service, credit reports
- https://naborly.com: Tenant screening you can trust. They use AI to help landlords automatically and securely verify their tenant's identity, income, and employment, while also providing a complete credit report and criminal background check absolutely free
- YouTube: http://youtube.com/revnyou: A great resource, but be sure you are getting quality content. The channel **RevNyou** is a *great* channel to follow and subscribe to.
- www.cmhc-schl.gc.ca: Canada Mortgage and Housing Corporation
- www.statscan.gc.ca: Statistics Canada
- www.rentometer.com: Look up rents in an area
- www.biggerpockets.com: Tons of resources for free
- www.messymanager.com: Download the free book *Messy Manager*

Books

- *More than Cashflow* by Julie Broad
- *Secrets of the Canadian Real Estate Cycle* by Don R. Campbell
- *97 Tips for Canadian Real Estate Investors* by Don R. Campbell
- *Real Estate Joint Ventures* by Don R. Campbell
- *Renos to Riches* by Ian Szabo
- *Fix & Flip* by Mark Loeffler and Ian Szabo
- *Rich Dad Poor Dad* by Robert Kiyosaki

- *The Book on Managing Rental Property* by Brandon & Heather Turner
- *The E Myth* by Michael E. Greber
- *Think and Grow Rich* by Napoleon Hill
- T*he Miracle Morning* by Hal Elrod
- *The Brand New You* by Julie Broad
- *Never Split the Difference* by Chris Voss
- *The 7 Habits of Highly Effective People* by Stephen Covey
- *Eat That Frog* by Brian Tracy
- *The 5 Second Rule* by Mel Robbins
- *Start with Why* by Simon Sinek
- *The 10X Rule* by Grant Cardone
- *Pitch Anything* by Oren Klaff
- *Canadian Real Estate Wealth Magazine*

Memberships and Groups

- REIN Canada
- Landlords Anonymous BC: active Facebook group for BC
- TheREinvestors
- Local real estate investors groups near you

Add more as you find them here:

_____

_____

Personal Development

This will vary widely, depending on where you are on this journey. A great author to follow regarding changing your mindset is, of course, **Tony Robbins**. He has various courses from self-discovery to business mastery, and everything in between. For several decades, this man has been the pinnacle of self-development and mindset, and I highly recommend attending one of his seminars. And if you are unable to, at least start to follow him on YouTube and other platforms, as there is a lot of free content that he shares.

Then there is **Don. R. Campbell (the legend)**. If you saw him, you would think he is a nerd (his words), and you would be right. But he really puts investing in real estate into perspective, and also elaborates on what is going on in the world that affects real estate.

Also, if you get the chance, get to an **ACRE** (Authentic Canadian Real Estate) event from REIN (Real Estate Investment Network) for some great mind-shifting.

Business Tools

- Mile-IQ App: Great for recording mileage and runs without you thinking about it.
- Ozone machine for getting rid of odors. Great for freshening up the place in-between tenants, or at other times: https://www.odorfreemachines.com/villa-3000/
- Cam-to-Plan: An App to help measure the room sizes and provide a floor plan. Great for renovations and for getting measurements for flooring, etc.
- Tiny Scanner: Take pictures and turn them into PDFs. Great for scanning documents and emailing—something you will do a lot of if you are in property management.

For an extensive list of forms, you can go to our website and download them for free, using the code *tenantsareclients2* at the checkout.

Here is an example of some of the checklists we use:

New Property Acquisition Checklist 1A

Address: _____

_____

House Type:

Single Family Detached; Townhouse; Apartment; Suite; Duplex; Other

Remember that this is the start of profiling your tenant

Currently rented: (Please circle)   YES   NO

If yes, current rent: $_____ (Confirm and make sure you have all the supporting paperwork.)

Market Rent for similar properties: $_____ (Use online resources to verify…)

Closest Schools: _____

_____

Closest Shops: _____

_____

This should be groceries, shops of interest such as drug stores, local convenience stores, etc. (not just "Bill's Plumbing")

Current Heat: _____

Average Cost of Hydro: _____

Gas $_____ Oil_____

Double glazed: YES   NO

Parking: YES   NO

If yes, how many vehicles?

Garage: YES   NO

If yes, detached?   YES   NO

Current Owner: _____

Current Owner EMERGENCY CONTACT: This is more for if you are joint ventured on the property so you can reach them quickly in the case of, well, an emergency!_____

Property Description: Bedrooms:_____ Bathrooms:_____

Living Room: _____ Dining Room: _____

Basement: Y / N Finished   Y / N Height:_____

Yard: Y / N   Fenced: Y / N   Flooring type:_____

Wall finish and colors: _____ *If you can, get the details of the types of paints, and places to purchase as well, if available, for touch ups, if required.*

Take pictures of the following and tick to confirm complete (use slight panoramic on phone, if possible):

- Front House   ☐
- Rear House   ☐
- Entrance from 6-10 feet away   ☐
- Entrance from front doorway   ☐
- Living room   ☐

- Kitchen ☐
- Bedroom(s) ☐
- Bathroom(s) ☐
- Back yard from house ☐
- Front yard from house ☐

Notes: _____

_____

_____

From this checklist, we can then write the advert that will be aimed at a certain profile of tenant, and when you are writing your adverts, you can too. What you must not do is discriminate in your adverts; for example, "Single people only" or "NO Kids," as this can land you in very hot water or a human rights trial—which gets expensive. We discuss this further in previous chapters.

Checklist 2B Tenant Screening

Tenant screening is a crucial part of finding a quality tenant, and it requires you to be a detective. Or follow these procedures and decide based on a standard set of questions and scoring. In the adverts, do not put your cell number; instead, have them do an action like email you with their cell number and the times you can call, and stating which house they are looking at, etc. (checklist 1C). These are simple instructions to follow and if they can't follow them, instructions for things like rent are also unlikely to be followed. This is the first stage before calling them.

1=Yes   **2=Maybe/Partly**   **3=No/Don't know**

- Did the applicant comply with the instructions in the advert?   1 2 3

- Does the applicant have social profiles you can see?   1 2 3

- Are the profiles suitable for whom you want to rent to?   1 2 3

- Does the applicant have a cell phone?   1 2 3

- Is the applicant connected to any *good* people you know?   1 2 3

Scores: 5-10 Good   10-12 Caution   12-15 Extreme Caution

The above is just to serve as a guide for calling people and then getting more information *before* viewing. Neither is yet *bad*, unless their social profiles raise a huge red flag; for example, illegal drug use, racism, etc. Use this sheet as a guide when you call them, and use checklist 2C as the phone interview checklist.

Checklist completed by: _____

print & sign

Your notes: _____

_____

_____

_____

Checklist 2C Tenant Phone Screening

Tenant phone screening is one of the best ways to get a feel for the tenant and how you can communicate with them. I never show a house to a person unless we have spoken on the phone or I know them from previous rentals. Below is a set of questions with a score for each; the score will help you remove emotions from the decision so you can get the best possible score for the house. Explain that you have a set of questions to ask before viewing.

1= Good   2= Partly/Okay   3= Don't know/Bad

- Was the person polite when answering the   1   2   3
  phone?

  Questions to ask:

- What type of house are you looking for?   1   2   3
  (Does this match your unit?)
  Notes:

- Why are you looking for this type of house?   1   2   3
  Notes:

- Why are you leaving your current residence?   1   2   3
  Notes:

- What was your current landlord like? (Do   1   2   3
  they complain?)
  Notes:

- What is your current rent? (Is this close to   1   2   3
  your price?)
  Notes:

- How are you going to afford this rent?   1   2   3
  Notes:

- Do you work, if yes where, if no why not?   1   2   3
  (Answer reasonable?)
  Notes:

- Who will be living in the house with you?   1   2   3
  Notes:

- Have you ever owned your own home?   1   2   3
  Notes:

- Have you ever been evicted from any rental   1   2   3
  unit for any reason?
  Notes:

- All our properties are no smoking prop-   1   2   3
  erties, no vaping or marijuana including
  medical, and if anyone wanted to do any
  of these they would have to leave the property. Would this be a problem for anyone
  staying at the property?
  Notes:

- If we have evidence of illegal drug use in   1   2   3
  our properties, notice will be given immediately. We want to make sure our homes
  are safe for the tenants, the neighbours,
  and anyone involved in managing the
  property. Will this be a problem for anyone visiting the property or staying at the
  property?
  Notes:

- Do you volunteer or are you a member of   1   2   3
  any community clubs or events?
  Notes:

- Do you have kids that live with you part   1   2   3
  time or full time?
  Notes:

Remember that these are guides for the viewing only, and not to
be used solely for the purpose of renting or not renting. This gives
you a base for communication with the potential tenant. A high
score does not necessarily mean a better tenant than a low score; it
just means investigate a lot further.

Scores:

16-25	25-32 Investigate	33+ Investigate a lot further
Good	further	and verify what is said

The above is meant to serve as a guide for communicating with
people. Some other questions I ask sometimes to verify but not
score further are:

- Would you mind if we did a credit history check, and would it have anything unusual?
- Would you mind if we did a police criminal record check, and is there anything we should know? (We do not actually do these; however, the question does two things: it makes shifty people not show up at the viewing and thus eliminate themselves; OR "John" tells you about when he got busted smoking pot in college. Either way, you get more information.) Be careful when asking this.
- I see you know *(Insert common friend if you have one off Facebook, for example)*—how do you know them? Again, be careful around certain privacy laws in your jurisdiction.
- This is all great information and the viewing times are: (insert viewing times). We will have applications to fill out on site. Do you think that you will be attending?

Always allow them to complete the application and to come to the group viewing—don't ever give them a reason to say you discriminated against them, even if you already know you do not want to rent to them.

At the viewings, I ask some of the same questions again, claiming I had so many applicants that I have forgotten who said what. Then I make sure to check what they say *now* compared to the answers they gave previously (have the sheets with you so you can check them). If there are any discrepancies, it's a red flag.

The application form also asks some of the same questions; again, verify that their answers are consistent. Then use all three forms to make an informed decision about the tenant, their ability to afford the place, and their ability to look after it and keep it in great condition.